FROM THE
PASTOR'S DAUGHTER

FROM THE PASTOR'S DAUGHTER

A TESTIMONY OF LIFE IN THE MINISTRY THROUGH THE EYES OF THE PASTOR'S CHILD

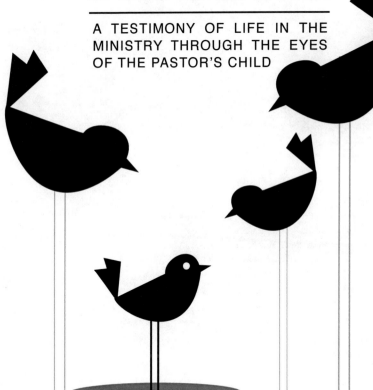

Aundria H. Hawkins Ford

Tate Publishing & *Enterprises*

From the Pastor's Daughter
Copyright © 2009 by Aundria H. Hawkins Ford. All rights reserved.

No part of this publication may be reproduced, stored in a retrieval system or transmitted in any way by any means, electronic, mechanical, photocopy, recording or otherwise without the prior permission of the author except as provided by USA copyright law.

The opinions expressed by the author are not necessarily those of Tate Publishing, LLC.

Published by Tate Publishing & Enterprises, LLC
127 E. Trade Center Terrace | Mustang, Oklahoma 73064 USA
1.888.361.9473 | www.tatepublishing.com

Tate Publishing is committed to excellence in the publishing industry. The company reflects the philosophy established by the founders, based on Psalm 68:11,
"The Lord gave the word and great was the company of those who published it."

Book design copyright © 2009 by Tate Publishing, LLC. All rights reserved.
Cover design by Kandi Evans
Interior design by Blake Brasor

Published in the United States of America

ISBN: 978-1-60799-803-7
1. Religion, Christian Life, Social Issues
2. Religion, Christian Life, Inspirational
09.10.15

Dedication

Dedicated to the life and legacy of
Dr. Eddie L. Hawkins, Senior Pastor

To My Father, My Pastor, My Hero...

No words within my vocabulary can begin to express how proud I am of you and what an honor it is to have you as my dad. I'm so thankful you're my father, and that God has given me so many years with you. There were countless times during the ministry years that I needed you, not as my pastor, but as my father. Thank you for being just that. It is said that girls gain their sense of self from their fathers. I concur, because the strongest parts of me come from you. Thank you for positively shaping my life. Even more, thank you for exemplifying what a Godly man should be. Daddy, you've set an awesome standard that I will forever strive to maintain. Without knowing it, you taught me how to choose and to be chosen. You taught me (or rather showed me) the essence of love: love in marriage, love in family, and love in ministry. You equipped me well for all that life has in store. You paved the way for my success, both spiritually and practically, and I am eternally grateful. Know that I admire you. I adore you. I will reverence you always.

Despite human frailties, in spite of the innumerable ministry demands, you found a way to extend yourself just enough to your family. I didn't always understand or appreciate your way, yet today it has become my sanctuary. Because of your love, I can more easily accept the love of Christ. Because of your fatherhood, I can better relate to him as a Father. Because of your example, I count it a privilege to serve him as his child.

My prayer is that you have the opportunity to read the finished work of this book, for you are responsible for its conception. I hope to honor your legacy through its completion.

The glory of children is their father!
Proverbs 17:6b (KJV)

To My Mother, My Heroine, My Eternal Best Friend…

Though it wasn't destined for you to share in this season of our lives, my whole heart wishes that you were here. This is yet another significant part of my journey without you, yet because of the imprint you've left on my life, I feel your presence each step of the way. You're ever present in my heart; your spirit abides with me; your person endures as my role model; your memory remains my consolation. Thank you for loving me unconditionally. Thank you for our relationship. Thank you for nurturing me so completely and for preparing me for my life in ministry, my role in marriage, my responsibility as a mother, and for my destiny, by God's design! Most of all, thank you, Mom, for your resounding assurance of God's plan.

You perfectly exemplified what a pastor's wife, a Christian wife should be. As I navigate my way through life in ministry, I pray constantly that the Lord will enable me to recall every bit of wisdom you shared and every instruction you gave in this regard. You laid a solid foundation for us to build upon. Your children were trained up in the way of the Lord and will not ultimately depart . Your family is thankful for each day that God gave us with you, and we'll continue to grow from the roots that you so faithfully planted.

As I prayerfully searched for the words to put on the pages of this book, I realized how each moment with you laid a durable cornerstone for all the seasons of my life. And while I transparently share these seasons with the world, I draw on strength, courage, and wisdom acquired during my thirty-two remarkable years with you. I will forever recall your fervent prayers that the Lord would have his way in the lives of your children, and that he would cause us to submit to his will. Know that your prayers have been answered. His will is being accomplished in each of our lives. We love you, Mom.

> Forsake not the law of thy mother.
> Proverbs 6:20b (KJV)

To My Husband...

Our brief journey thus far has been incredible. I cherish the perspective you bring to my life. Thank you for your encouragement. Thank you for seeing something in me that I couldn't see, and for giving me the courage to move beyond my fears. Thank you for loving me into each tomorrow. Thank you for entering each new day by my side, for sharing my dreams, for giving me stability, for shaping my wings! I love you.

To Erica Lau'ren... my child, my motivation, my blessing

You are the instrument that God used to affect a sweeter melody in my life; the tool that he used to help mold me into the person that he would have me to be. I can't imagine what my existence would be without you. Thank God that you're here. I urge you to forever honor our existing legacy, and to allow the Lord to order your steps as you create a wonderful new legacy of your own. Be reminded, For I know the plans I have for you, says the Lord; plans for good and not for evil, to give you a future and a hope.

(Jeremiah 29:11, RSV)

TABLE OF CONTENTS

Foreword 11
Introduction 13
For the Sake of the Call 19
A Man of God, a Woman of Virtue 35
A House Divided Cannot Stand 55
The Separation Sacrifice 75
Under the Spotlight 85
A Necessary Condition 119
Pain with a Purpose 133
Recovery, Spiritual Maturity, and Restoration 163
So That Not One of These Little Ones Perish 175
Ministry Oriented or Christ Oriented? 183
The Legacy 191

Foreword

When first inspired to write this book, I was nineteen years old and on an involuntary sabbatical from ministry. I'd fallen into public sin. At that time, my inspiration to write was fueled by all of the hardship, sacrifice, cost, and emotional devastation associated with being a daughter of a very spiritual pastor in a very secular world. I had no idea that my pain was part of a necessary process that would begin a journey toward a personal relationship with Christ. Nor could I have ever fathomed the place where I would be almost twenty years later when that relationship would fine tune the vision, and cause my life experiences to be translated from the sacred places of my heart to the very public pages of this book.

At nineteen, my objective was to vent frustrations with a life that I didn't choose, and didn't necessarily want. Now a little wiser, a lot stronger, with a substantial increase in Godly perspective, the Lord has shown me that my trials have become my testimony, and my testimony will become another's encouragement. More important, the Lord taught me that in this day and age, it is not only critical that the body of Christ understands the sovereignty of God, but that they learn to live by faith, trusting that he is in emphatically control and that he has the best interest of his children, and his church, at heart.

Prayerfully, this book will help reinforce our reverence for true men of God, and help distinguish them by their lives, their faith, their role in the family, and their fruit. Hopefully, it will also provide frequently overlooked insight into the lives of the first families of ministry: the call, the cost, the covering, and the crown effectually associated with their roles in, and out, of the church. Finally, it will prayerfully serve as encouragement to those who are weighed down by the issues of life while managing their public persona. I challenge you to see yourself only through God's eyes. Trust me, the outlook is much better through Divine vision!

May God bless each reader for supporting this work. May he draw you closer to himself, give you the boldness to share the Gospel of Jesus Christ, and give you the transparency to encourage others with your testimony.

> Let the words of my mouth and the meditation of my heart be acceptable in thy sight,
> O Lord, my strength and my redeemer.
>
> Psalms 19:14 (KJV)

Introduction

If I'm no longer the pastor's daughter, then who am I? That's the poignant question I pondered continuously as we prepared for my father's impending retirement from more than half a century in the ministry. When I opened my eyes at birth, I did so as the pastor's daughter and member of the first family of Good Shepherd Baptist Church. We weren't appointed to this role, we were born and bred into it. It's all we've ever known. It's who we've always been. And so now in the weeks, days, and moments directly preceding our exodus out of our only home church and lifetime roles, I struggled to imagine what life would be like the day after we were no longer who we'd always been. And if we never experienced the process of transitioning *into* this place, how on earth could we know how to transition *out*?

What will Sundays now feel like? What will church homelessness feel like? What will the process of starting over in a new church, a new ministry, a new beginning, a new life, a new existence, a new position, a new identity all mean? If not the choir director, if not a ministry leader, without the pain, pressure, and chaos of perpetually being at the center of it all, then who am I? And if Dad is no longer the pastor, then I'm no longer the pastor's daughter. But how could that be? After all, that's all I've ever been! The office at the entrance of the church has always been his, for more than fifty years, for all my life, it's been his! The private restroom behind the pulpit - his! The parking space in the circle of the lot-his! The seat in the pulpithis! The seat on the front row-ours! He has been Pastor Hawkins since the ministry's inception, and since our family's conception. So if none of this will be so tomorrow, then what will tomorrow be?

I've never so much as visited another church unless my father was preaching there, or if our choir was asked to minister in music. We traveled all over the country to support him as he led various church revivals, conducted ministry workshops, taught pastoral classes, and served as guest speaker in worship services. Yet never have I visited other congregations just for sake of fellowship. Never in my life have I gone through the process of seeking a church home, examining another church body, or joining another church. Never have I experienced church homelessness. Never have I known what it's like *not* to be part of a church body, *not* to attend church regularly, *not* to participate in ministry, and *not* to be a ministry leader. We were born and bred. What's it like to be a musician or director for hire at a church where you don't belong, as opposed to serving at your home church as part of your family's call? What is it like to be a member of a body pastored by someone other than your dad? What is it like to be a bench member, to exist in the background, to have no knowledge of what goes on behind the scenes or in the upper room so to speak? To whom would I now be accountable? How will I conduct myself when no one is watching? How will I live outside of the proverbial *glass house*'? If not under the magnifying glass, how will my life be evaluated? Most fascinating of all, what would it be like to go to church and simply worship; to engage in undistracted, unadulterated worship. Imagine attending church not to minister, but rather for the sole purpose of *being ministered to*.

Most of us wear multiple hats. Some of us carry a multitude of titles. We're mom or dad, co-worker, teacher, neighbor, mentor, ministry leader, child, sibling, professional, and so on. But within all of these titles, under all of the various hats, and amidst all of our realms of significance exists a single facet of our existence that serves as our primary identity, our paramount purpose, our essence, our *who am I*... It's this identity that gives us our greatest significance, establishes our self-worth, and sets the stage for our performance in life. It's our most compelling reason for what we do, how we interact with the world, and to what extent we are accountable for our actions. It's our core, our center, our nucleus, our self. For some that single identity is being a wife. For others it's being CEO of a prominent company. Still others identify themselves as parents, with their children serving as their definition.

Me? I'm the pastor's daughter. All of my other roles and hats fell under this distinction. The funny thing is, I didn't realize that this was my fundamental identity until the time came to relinquish it! I never considered how much being the pastor's daughter defined me, or the extent to which it served as the foundation for most of what I did, and everything that I was. It not only determined what I chose to do, but what I chose *not* to do. It guided my choices, dictated my decisions, shaped my self-perception (positive and negative), influenced my opinions, established my value system, determined my doctrinal position, and molded my inner person. It even influenced my relationship with Christ, securing my faith yet often hindering my fellowship (we'll explore that irony more in later chapters).

Now, after a lifetime of taking for granted the pertinence, the blessing, the privilege, the honor, the high call, and the spiritual charge associated with this identity, the rubber finally meets the road (as my father would always say). It is now that my true character will be revealed, not my reputation, not the person that I am when all the world is watching, but rather the testimony that I maintain in the solitude of my daily life. It is now time to shed the old titles. It's now time to come from behind the vale, sanctity, definition and covering of the first family, and finally learn who, *in fact*, and who, *in Christ*, I really am. It is now that my faith is truly tested, and my Godly character is fully shaped.

All that I share herein is not for your entertainment (although entertaining some of it may very well be!), nor to arm you with ammunition for attacks against my family, or the family of Christ. It is rather to give account of ministerial life, to honor my Savior, and to pay homage to my father, my pastor, who made this life journey a very blessed one.

Father God, forgive me for missing so many opportunities to maximize this appointment to glorify you and further your kingdom. I pray and trust that you will be ever glorified hereafter.

> My eager desire and hope is that I may never be ashamed,
> but that I may boldly honor Christ in my person.
> Philippians 1:20 (paraphrased)

For the Sake of the Call

To lay the foundation for this book, it is crucial that I establish a framework in the first two chapters for readers to fully conceptualize ministerial life, and the common experiences therein.

In an age where so many proclaim their call to preach the Word of God and pastor the body of Christ, my heart grieves the loss of Godly reverence, integrity, and accountability in present-day ministry. In too many cases, today's call seems to stem more from the desire of an anticipated lifestyle and position of influence than a true encounter with Christ. We have an influx of men, women, and others who are operating under a self-summoning, and as a result, set their own standards for their ministries and their lives. Unfortunately, these standards are often contrary to the Word of God, and fail to serve the spiritual best interest of his people.

This is not to say that there aren't those well-doers who make a positive difference by significantly impacting their communities and giving people a sense of hope that would have otherwise been hopeless. Yet, there is a profound difference between good work and kingdom work.

You see, the only objective Christ had when he came to earth was to build his kingdom. The Bible says that he came to seek and to save that which was lost (Luke 19:10, KJV). He operated not for individual or community good, not to further a self-designed agenda, but rather according to the express will and purpose of the Father. His was a mission of introducing the world to salvation, preparing them for their role in the body of Christ, and training them for the task of glorifying God by building the kingdom of God.

That's it! Christ had no interest in drawing people to himself for the sake of fame, fortune, or significance. He didn't take on the lifestyle, characteristics, and appearance of the secular world in order to point them toward the gospel: no break dancing in the synagogue to Jewish re-mixes; no changing the lyrics to Pharaoh's secular hits to make them church songs; no wearing low-riding jeans and white tees like the young folks to get their attention and fit in; no promises of material wealth to gain a massive following; no milking the gentiles for their hard-earned money to build a fly new manger and pimp' his donkey ride; no gimmicks; no watered-down truth; no rhymes; no spin; no clever packaging; no regard for pleasing the people. His ministry was focused and his mission was clear. Christ came to introduce us to salvation. The Father allowed the Son to sacrifice his life for our salvation-regardless of whether or not we'd accept him. He died on Calvary as a means for us to obtain a birthright into the kingdom. He rose from the dead to pave the road to our victory. The crowd didn't always like who he was, or what he had to say, and they certainly didn't always like the way that he said it. He proclaimed the un-compromised gospel, and lived his proclamation without exception. When others expressed a desire to join the ministry or become his disciples, he advised them of the cost. He didn't bait them with promises of wealth, health, or any gain other than eternal life with Jesus Christ.

Did Christ make it clear that the cattle on a thousand hills are his? Absolutely! Did he promise that the same would be obtained by everyone that followed him, lived right, and did his will, in this lifetime? Absolutely not. Our guaranteed inheritance is heaven. Certainly the benefits of living a godly life are having his hand in our midst, and avoiding much of the self-inflicted pain that comes from disobedience. But the sole purpose of our creation is not based on what he can do for us, but rather what we can do for him! We somehow get that completely *twisted*, as the young folks say. All that we are blessed with on earth is by the grace of God, according to his divine or permissive will. All that we have, all that we are, all that we ever hope to be, is by his grace and is permitted solely for the sake of his glory. He loves us enough to give us more than we deserve, and more than what we give him in return.

Yet, that's not what we hear today. That's not what we're taught, and that's not the premise upon which so many of our clergymen enter the pastoral profession. Lacking today are the characteristics of a true call such as self-sacrifice, commitment, accountability, exemplary Christian living, a heart for people, a heart for service, a genuine lifestyle of worship, knowledge *and* application of the Word, and an intimate relationship with Christ which is evidenced by one's walk. Churches have lost credibility within our society. Pastorship has become a sought-after occupation, rather than a sacrificial mandate from God. It has become more of a vehicle for power, position, notoriety, and financial success than a method of getting the Gospel of Jesus Christ to the world. It's ten minutes to twelve on the clock of life, yet we're playing with souls as if Christ isn't coming back. Ladies and gentlemen, he *is* coming back, and each believer (pastor or not) is charged with the mission of getting the gospel message to the world. We not only have to speak it, but we must also live it in a way that preserves the reputation of Christianity and draws others into the fold.

Although we are called to be fruit inspectors in this regard, and to be aware of false prophets in these latter days, my point here is not condemn ministers, but rather to clearly distinguish the true call of the pastor. That's the perspective of this book. The unsolicited, rarely preferred call from the Lord for his servant to commit his entire existence to the express will of God, and to dedicate his life wholly, fully, and unconditionally, to ministry. This is the only perspective of ministerial life that I can intelligently speak of, as it is the only ministerial life I know. I have no insider knowledge of ministry as a business, as a commercial venture, as a political platform, or as any other marketable tool for financial success. I know only of ministry where the heart of God meets the heart of people, and therein he accomplishes his plan.

For thirty-nine years I have had the absolute privilege of seeing first hand what a true call to the ministry looks like. I've observed, first hand, this call on the life of a true man of God, my father.

The Call of the Pastor

My father was an unlikely candidate for pastorship from man's perspective. He was born in Studgard, Arkansas, to an African American man and a beautiful Filipino woman. His mother became sick and died while he was a very young child. At that time, his father moved the family to Flint, Michigan, so that my dad's elder sisters could assist in the rearing of he and two other brothers. His father went home to be with the Lord a short time later during my dad's mid-teen years. Having lost both parents and received little emotional support from his half sisters, a tremendous void was left in his life. To further agitate matters, he was a somewhat rambunctious child who landed in trouble from time to time (he didn't have to be led into temptation, he found it all by himself!). As a result, he lived under the weight of his family's negative prediction on his life:that his defiant ways would result in his death before the age of twenty-one. Can you imagine your loved ones telling you that you'd be dead by twenty-one? What does that do to a young man when, in the midst of tremendous grief, such an negative cloud-a forecast straight from the pits of hell-is draped over his youthful life? Thank God, the prediction was neither prophetic nor self-fulfilling. Instead, God had a very different plan for my dad's life. In fact, he had already anointed my father for kingdom work.

Dad joined the United States Marine Corp. at seventeen years old as a means for practical support, guidance, and a perhaps sense of belonging. This was clearly the hand of God, because it was in the Marine Corp. that he gained life skills for survival and learned the essence of manhood. The Marines gave him definition, confidence, integrity, and a newfound esteem that not only groomed him for future leadership, but began to establish a track record of success. Note that it was during his tour of duty in the Marine Corp. that he earned the title as featherweight boxing champion, again further reinforcing his confidence and serving as a symbolic representation of the fights that he would engage in, and be victorious in, throughout his ministry life. *That revelation just came to me, I wonder if he ever thought of that?* Clearly, this was his season of restoration. From a human perspective, it was the beginning of his call.

After leaving the military, he briefly returned to his hometown in Flint, Michigan, where, unknown to him, God's plan was about to unfold. He attended a revival where the late Dr. Walter Banks, a prominent pastor, author, teacher, and servant of God, was speaking. Dr. Banks spent time with him after the service and apparently saw my father through God's eyes.

Let me pause and place emphasis on this point because it's very compelling: this Man of God saw my father through *God's* eyes. The Bible says that, man looketh on the outward appearance, but the Lord looketh on the heart (1 Samuel 16:7, KJV). We quote that scripture all the time, yet we continue to assess ourselves, and others, through a secular lens. We, too, make inaccurate predictions and faulty assessments because we don't prayerfully seek the Lord's view of the situation. Instead, we draw our own conclusions based on what that person, thing, or situation is right now rather than where, by the grace of God, he/she/it has the potential to be. No one saw a king in David ... But God. No one saw a leader in Joseph ... But God. No one saw a witness in the harlot at the well ... But

God. No one may see the awesome ministry, task, or role that the Lord is grooming you for, or how it will effectually impact his kingdom ... But God! Don't make the mistake of underestimating the proven reality that God can use anyone, anytime, in any scenario, for his glory. He delights in taking something ordinary and making it extraordinary. He specializes in defying the impossible and accomplishing beyond what man can dare to think, dream, or imagine. Know that you are as much a candidate for his divine orchestration as anyone else. Availability trumps ability, he'll respond to a willing vessel every time!

So, back to the story. Dr. Banks encouraged my father to attend a seminary Bible college in Cleveland, Ohio. It was in Cleveland that the Lord took my father through his necessary condition, a process that I explore in great detail in later chapters. For him, this process included a period of exclusion, extreme poverty, social depravity, failing health, depression, and fear. It was at this place that he encountered Jehovah-jireh, the Lord as provider; Jehovah-shalom, the Lord as peace; Jehovah-raphia, the Lord God as healer. When he arrived in Cleveland for seminary school, he knew no one. He took residence in a second floor room of a house owned by a Christian woman who also saw something special in him. I recall my father emotionally describing this period of his life: how absolutely destitute he was; how he'd go to bed at night so hungry yet not knowing where his next meal or provision would come from. He vividly describes his state of depression and physical illness to the point of feeling that he wouldn't make it through the night. It was during this time that he would reminisce the days when his own father was alive. He had a clear memory of his father being in the privacy of his bedroom, with the door cracked enough for my dad to see him, reading the Word of God. He recalled tears dropped from his father's eyes onto the pages of the Bible. He recalled watching his father pray. This memory was powerful during my dad's wilderness experience. Now alone and deeply depressed, he, too, opened his Bible and began to read the Word; he, too, cried out to the Lord as the tears dropped from his eyes to the pages; and he, too, encountered the Lord in a very personal, intimate, way. It was at that moment that he embraced the scripture, I will never leave thee, nor forsake thee (Hebrews 13:5, KJV). It was then that he realized that there was a calling on his life. He asked God right then and there to reveal the plan for his life, and to keep him in the process until that plan was fulfilled. That prayer was answered. God kept him, and God blessed him.

He successfully completed pastoral training at the seminary. Immediately thereafter, he was asked to assist in the organization of, and serve as director for, what would be known as the Good Shepherd Bible Center. What started out as midweek Bible study and Sunday school soon grew into a small church, Good Shepherd Baptist Church. He served as founding pastor from 1957 through the present publishing of this book more than fifty years later. The sequence of events that led to and followed his entrance into the ministry reflected a purposeful design on his life that only Christ could have engineered. The impact of my father's ministry evidences a true call, and the fruits of a wholehearted response.

The Call of the Family

It may seem strange, even pretentious, to dedicate a section of this book to the *family's call*. After all, what does the family have to do with the call? I'm glad you asked! Much like almost any public office, when the leader is appointed, the entire family becomes subject to the appointment. Whether voluntarily or under duress, we too become 100-percent stakeholders in the venture. Allow me to pause and point out that I, for one, initially objected to this appointment. I did not sign on for this tour of duty. I was drafted against my will, under duress, and in violation of my inalienable rights. After all, there is no life, liberty, or pursuit of happiness when your dad is the pastor.

The pastor's family, by association, becomes benefactors and/or casualties of the call. Having interviewed countless pastoral families, I've encountered only a small number whose lives on the inside are anywhere near as charmed as what appears on the outside. Not many of my fellow first families would have readily elected their role if given the option. In fact, most would trade one year of their lives under the church spotlight for even one day of peace, tranquility, and an anonymous existence. The reason? The role and responsibilities of leadership are not exclusive to the head. A truly successful leader-any public leader-has commissioned his family for the call, delegated a host of responsibilities, and charged them with ever-rising levels of accountability. In society, this is necessary so that the family will not undermine the authority of the leader or cause embarrassment to the office. In ministry, this is necessary for them to be spiritually profitable to the ministry and to the body of Christ. You see, the pastor's family undergoes a mandatory forfeiture of individual rights. My mother used to quote the scripture, all things are lawful, but not all things are expedient; all things are permissible, but I will not be brought under the power of any (1 Corinthians 6:12, RSV). This was her tactful way of saying 'you have no right to exercise your rights!' In our household, children exercising personal rights like kids do today was neither advisable, nor safe! There was very little mediation when we rebelliously exercised our freedom consequences were swift and severe. No due process, no public defender, no innocent until proven guilty. No sparing of the rod. It's funny now that I think of it, that's probably what made me want to pursue a career in law… to regain my childhood rights.

The pastoral family's understanding of their call is essential to the success of the work. Foremost, the leader's wife holds what is undeniably the most significant role in office as a support to the head. Her role as partner in marriage is immediately expanded to partner in business, in public, and in this case, in ministry. His life becomes her life; his fears become her fears; his burdens become her burdens; his success becomes her success; his failures become her failures; his reputation becomes her reputation; his values become her values; his position becomes her position; and his sacrifice, too, becomes hers. Whatever she did before, whoever she was before, now moot. She immediately transforms into the wife of the public figure, and she becomes an extension of him. Whether she masters this role (as my mother certainly did), or whether she falls miserably short, her implied assignment, and the expectation that she fulfill it, doesn't change. She bears the full responsibility, burden, and all related implications of the appointment. In this respect, she, too, receives and accepts the call.

Next, the leader's children are subjects of the appointment. We don't get a say so in whether our parent become a public figure. We don't get to decide whether we want to be public kids. We aren't given the opportunity to opt out of the situation and maintain our status quo. We're appointed by default. We answer without option. And in many cases, we're born into an already in-force way of life that has a prescribed outline of how we must live, behave, respond, react, appear, and exist.

Such was my fate. Having been born into the ministry, this life is all I ever knew. The church members knew me before I knew myself. And the mass expectations for the person that I would be were already established when I entered the world. Unfortunately, no one clued me in on those expectations, so imagine their surprise, and disappointment, when I failed to measure up to *their* dreams. I'll share more about this in coming chapters.

Yet I believe that God creates atmospheres that are favorable for pastoral families to assume their roles and settle into their very unique world. This is not to say that he perfects us, nor is it to imply that we are always ready, willing participants. But somewhere in the process, he begins a collective and individual work in our lives that helps prepare us for our ministerial roles. Our success is wholly a function of our obedience and submission to his will.

My initial comparisons of many present-day, self-summoned ministers to those called by the Lord lacked emphasis on the most important distinction: *when the call is from the Lord, everything is placed on the altar*. Everything is sacrificed for the sake of the call. The New Testament of the Bible denotes several instances where people said they wanted to follow Christ and be a part of his ministry. His stipulation was that they forsake everything else, take up their cross, and wholeheartedly follow him. Those with ulterior motives typically gave excuses as to why they couldn't do so at that time: they had to tend to other matters; they couldn't give up their possessions (their bling bling) just yet; they couldn't fully commit at this time. Remember the New Testament man who wanted to bury his father before following Chris-this father who hadn't died yet? And then there were those who wanted to finish up projects or exhaust all other options, then come aboard at a more convenient time. Remember Peter, who declared he had the Savior's back and would stick with Jesus forever? Well, Jesus must have finally been fed up with broken promises, because he blessed Peter out immediately. He told Peter, *Man, there you go again, quit frontin'! You're gonna bounce before nightfall* (I paraphrased, of course. Feel free to read the actual King James Version in Matthew 26:75).

Even in biblical days, Christ was interested in those who had a true heart for his kingdom and a countenance of servitude. What most folks didn't realize was that all blessings come directly from God. In denying all else, taking up their cross, and following him, they would not only experience true fulfillment, but their needs would be abundantly met and their bounty restored.

The true call to pastoral ministry requires a level of sacrifice that often makes the appointment unattractive from a human standpoint. Most pastors whom I've either interviewed or known personally over the years, who have dedicated their lives to preaching and teaching the

Word of God, were unanimous on one point: they initially resisted the call! Even their estimation of the required cost made them prefer to do something less sacrificial with their lives. It was only in obedience to the compelling Will of God that they ultimately hearkened to his voice and entered full time ministry. I gleamed from this that the mad rush to start churches and pastor flocks seen today has to be rooted in self-serving motives. Otherwise, there must be a very limited understanding of the cost associated with the call.

For my family, accepting the call meant anything *but* the good life. It meant charity dinners at the homes of church mothers when we couldn't afford our own; it meant government block cheese and butter (although grilled cheese sandwiches made from government cheese were quite delightful if you could get the cheese to melt!); it meant traveling to and fro in a temperamental station wagon donated to our family after being used for ten years by the original owner; it meant having a single thirteen-inch black and white television to be shared among four children until my eldest sister went to work and could afford a nineteen-inch color TV of her own; it meant hand-sown clothes where our dresses matched our brothers' pants; it meant getting paper, pencils, crayons and actual school supplies at the *back to school sale*, instead of a nice pair of Jordache Jeans (that was the Rockawear of my day). Beyond the material sacrifice, it meant not seeing our dad in the evening, because he was serving at the church. It meant not seeing our dad at school events, because he was serving at the church; it meant being subjected to sibling authority while Mom accompanied Dad for out-of-town revivals, workshops, and other ministry events; it meant attending a minimum of two church services each Sunday, and a variety of church events during the week, all the time; it meant our home phone ringing from six a.m. often until after midnight as if we were 911 dispatchers; it meant continual counseling sessions in our family room which always seemed to be scheduled while Speedracer was on TV; it meant that church came first; the members came first; sick and shut in came first; weddings came first; funerals came first; revivals came first; members came first; *ministry* came first. We were second-class citizens in our own homes, and seemingly second priority in our parents' lives. This is only the beginning of our cost for the sake of the call.

As I recently observed the historical election of President Barack Obama on television, my attention immediately went to his wife and family. I wondered how they felt. I wondered about all of the conversations that must have taken place in the Obama home in the years, months, weeks, and days prior to election day. I wondered if there was apprehension on Mrs. Obama's part, or what words they used to explain to their children how their lives would necessarily change. How would they transition from one world to the other? How would they weather the scrutiny, the perpetual spotlight, the storms? How would they manage the often unfair, and more often unrealistic, expectations of others? Clearly they were receptive of this call, but how could they know and how could they prepare for all that this call would mean? Their home would change. Their environment would change. Their friends, unfortunately, would change. Different schools, different church home, different affiliations, a new life. While their lives had never quite been private, now they were extreme public. They answered to a much higher office, a higher demand, a higher standard. Lord, help them endure the incredible standard! At that moment, my heart went out to them. I empathized with their young children. All that is within me wanted to reach out and hand them some support, some shelter from the impending storms, some encouragement. Instead, I prayed. Father, protect them, guide them, sustain them. And let them take on no less, and no more, than that which you give them the grace to bear, and that which will accomplish your will. Amen.

The old saying, To whom much is given, much is required, rang painfully true for our family. Much was given to us, and much was required of us. Yet, before you break out the violins, let me say in fairness that for everything we gave up, God later blessed us tenfold. And that was priceless. He covered us fully, at all times, in all seasons. He covered my father. He covered my mother. He covered my siblings. He covered me. And now, years later, he covered my child.

Only by God's divine appointment was I privileged to be raised in a pastoral family by God-fearing parents who understood the order of the family and their purpose in the kingdom. Through their example, I, too, have come to understand the purpose for which I was created: to glorify Christ in my person. I now understand that frequently quoted verse all things working together for good to them that love God and are called according to his purpose (Romans 8:28) means that the matters of my life are divinely orchestrated to ultimately effect my good and his glory. I understand now that his honor is preeminent. His glory is paramount. My blessings are for his glory; my trials are for his glory; my deliverance is for his glory; my gain is for his glory. He created me, chose me, equipped me, and positioned me to profit his kingdom. Being the pastor's daughter was not by chance. It was my destiny, by God's design. And for that, I am eternally grateful.

A Man of God, a Woman of Virtue

Portrait of a Pastor

If you want to know the true character of a pastor, ask his family!

As I've shared, my father was ordained in '57 as founding pastor of our church. Shortly thereafter in 1960, he married my mother, who was also a student at the seminary school my dad attended. They married six months after meeting one another and held their wedding ceremony in a funeral home. Hey, whatever works! They were married for forty-two years until my mom went home to glory. For more than four decades, they worked together to build the ministry, as husband and wife. Praise God. Over the years, he has counseled many pastors who were seeking to start new ministries, assuming a ministry in progress, or simply facing challenges in their church body. He always says that the most valuable advice he can ever give another pastor is: stay grounded in the Word of God, live a God-glorifying life, and preach the Word in and out of season. He understood that as time progressed, tides would drastically change. The temptation to conform to new world views and social norms would be ever present. He's seen countless fellow pastors fall victim to these ever-changing tides, and compromise or completely abandon their stance for Christ. The one thing that I count most extraordinary about my father is his consistent declaration of the Word of God. His faith is unwavering, and his doctrine never changed.

As children, my siblings and I were often annoyed by his consistency and what we considered to be an archaic position on secular issues versus Christian living. He didn't attend movies, social events that included dancing or drinking, or any function that presented even the slightest hint of impropriety. He took the scriptures at face value, 'avoid even the appearance of evil.' Well, geez Dad, if everything *appears* evil to you, then what else is left for us to do?! He wasn't mean or harsh, though, at all. He was absolutely hilarious. For example, he was ridiculously discriminating about what we watched on television or listened to on the radio. Nothing with cursing, sex, violence, or inappropriate attire was allowed. He would immediately change the channel if he heard or saw any of the above, which left us with the options of *Family Feud*, *Lost in Space*, *Sesame Street*, *The Jeffersons* (maybe), *That's My Mama* (perhaps), and *The Flintstones*. Oh, and *Speedracer*. Even the news was questionable, so he read *Time Magazine* instead. When my sister finally purchased a second TV with her own money, she ruled! We got to watch devilish shows like *Dallas*, *Dynasty*, and *Knots Landing*. Back then my parents would watch with us sometimes, and Dad would turn the channel if they so much as showed a bedroom or used the Lord's name in vain! Being the entrepreneur that I am by nature, I tried for years to get Dad to turn his incredible skills at billiards and checkers into part-time hustles that the family could benefit from. You know, put a little money on the table to get out of the hole, babies needed new shoes! I even tried to get things rolling by leaving a little change on the pool table in hopes of sending a subliminal message. To my dismay, he used it to send my brothers out for chips and cheese whiz so his guests could eat-for *free*. To this day, he still plays for silly benefits like fun, fellowship, and relaxation. That's my dad. Straight and narrow. Always has been, always will be.

I remember my father being apprehensive about my older brother living on college campus at Ohio State, warning him not to engage in any wild TV watching when he got there. We never quite figured out what constituted wild TV watching, but still today we jokingly warn my brother not to do it. In later college years, Dad objected to my brother moving off campus and into a wild condom. We laughed to the point of tears before we realized that he was serious and that he was referring to *condominiums*.

That's my father. He is nothing if not consistent. As a result, we always knew the standard in our home. We had no problem deciphering right from wrong, and we knew what would and would not be permitted. The standard was constant. We knew what my parents' position on any matter would be before we even asked. There was no guesswork involved. They were our standard in and out of the home. Before the term 'what would Jesus do,' it was 'what would Daddy do.' No kidding. He was our gauge when making judgment calls.

Because my father was at church most of the time, we had plenty of opportunity to get away with stuff. Note that I said *opportunity*. My parents were on child number three (me) before they slacked up enough for us to try our hand at mischief. Unfortunately, we just weren't very good at it. My older sister was so molded and had such endearment for my father that instead of enjoying the unsupervised time with friends, she would catch the three public transportation buses from her high school to our church and sit in my father's office until the evening activities started. By adolescence, my older brother had a little better handle on mischief than the rest of us. But even his shenanigans were mild by today's standard. Curfew seemed to be my major challenge. I simply needed a little clarity on the matter. The thing is, we were bad at deception. Our most ingenious plots were usually thwarted, not because we'd get caught, but because someone would break, turn state's evidence, and the rest would be history. With four kids in the house covering for each other, there is absolutely no reason anyone should ever get caught breaking curfew! All they had to do was come bring me the flashlight outside and help me push daddy's car up the driveway in neutral, then all the unnecessary drama of punishments and whippins could have been avoided. Besides, if my lovely siblings knew that I was going to come home late at the same time every night, help a sister out and be outside waiting with a cover-up plan! But no. They would fold every time for a government cheese sandwich and milk money. Wimps, I tell you! Over and over again, a sibling folds, state's evidence is turned, other sibling goes on lockdown... again. No teamwork, no moral support, just perpetual lockdown. But I digress.

Anyhow, we were ingrained. Even our friends held us to the standard. They would reprimand us for doing the same stuff they did because it somehow seemed worse when it was us. My brother's friends would be in the midst of a fight, and yell at him for joining in to help because he knew better. Once, my older sister urged my brother and me to run away, convincing us we would find a better life elsewhere (and her life at home would be better without us). We complied. We solicited two of my older brother's friends to give us, and our bags, a ride on their bikes to an undetermined destination (again, we were bad with mischief planning). About half way to nowhere, they turned their bikes around and started back toward home. Apparently, they feared being exposed by my father in the following Sunday's sermon. Funny thing was, they didn't even go to church! But that was our lives. We were sheltered. We were protected. Even when we didn't want to be, even in our wrongdoing, we were sheltered. Because my father trained us, my mother prayed for us, and the Lord covered us, and all the world seemingly knew it, we stood very little chance of success in the world of juvenile delinquency. Now I'm thankful.

Until the ministry could support our family, my father worked as a hospital orderly, then later at a bank, to earn our living and pay bills at church. Back then, that's how it worked. A founding pastor didn't profit from the church, he supported it! It's rumored that my mom worked at some point also, but I don't recall attending *take your daughter to work day* so it had to have been before my time. When I came along, my father had already been pastoring our church for more than twelve years. By then, he served as full-time pastor, and my mother as a full-time first lady, wife, and mother-in that order. We lived in a decent area, in a decent house most of my life, so I couldn't really see their struggle. But looking back, I realize how little we actually had by comparison, how much sacrifice there was, and how many years it took before they were comfortable enough to exhale. My parents weren't materialistic by any means. They were happy with the basics. My mom was frugal to a fault, so we had to master the barter system with our peers to get cool stuff. My dad was the most generous poor man we've ever met! He gave any extra money we had away. If he thought others needed it (as if we didn't), or if they asked, or if they happened to be in his presence on a day he had money, they were recipients. He kept enough to survive and gave the rest away. We tried relentlessly to make him understand that *we, ourselves,* were the needy, and that it's not politically or socially correct for needy people to support other needy people. That's not how the welfare system is designed to work. This logic irritated him. He yelled at us for even suggesting we were on welfare, called us ingrates, and gave away even more.

But he instilled in us a standard of generosity that we can't seem to shake. To this day, we all do the very same thing that we resented seeing him do as children. We finally grasped that he wasn't being taken advantage of; he was simply demonstrating his thankfulness and opening a door for others to come to Christ. Even in instances where others did take advantage, the Lord always seemed to bless him. Looking back, I guess we never really wanted for anything. I mean, we wanted stuff... stuff we didn't get. But we were never in need. Could it be that blessings come through our giving? Could it be that the Scriptures are correct, that when we give to the poor we lend to God?

Could it be that our duty as Christians is to demonstrate love through charity? *Could it be that God blesses us, not just for the sake of us being blessed, but so that we can be a blessing?* Could it be that the best way that we can evidence our thankfulness for all he has done is to, in turn, do for others, in obedience to him? Could it be that my father not only understood all of this, but he elected to teach by example so that his bratty kids would some day follow suit? We saw it, Dad. We learned it. We now live it.

Another absolute my father had was that the pastor should never handle the church's money. Don't laugh. I'm serious! I realize this is unheard of today, but it was one of the principles by which he lived. Not only did he refrain from ever touching church money, but he forbade his family from handling church funds as well. We weren't allowed on the counting committee; we weren't allowed to collect the offering in Sunday school; and we couldn't take up offering in prayer meeting unless we were the only options, and a deacon or security were present to oversee the basket. Mind you, some prayer meetings consisted only of us. We weren't even allowed to collect our own offering! It always amazed us to see Fortune 500 ministers on television because we couldn't figure out how they got past the deacons, trustees, and business office to get to the money. It never dawned on us that perhaps these offices didn't exist, and they simply took it. After all these years, Dad still won't touch the money. He accepts a fair salary for his service, a few fringe benefits (parking space, chicken, etc.), and that about sums it up. Fifty years. Same standard. God bless him!

What probably impressed me most growing up was my father's tireless reading of the Word of God. I'd frequently borrow one of his many Bibles for use at church for convenience sake, and as I turned the pages, I'd notice his markings of the date and time that he'd completed that section of scripture. All of his Bibles have multiple dates and times on the same passages of each page, because he's read the Bible through so often. He places high priority on devotional time and on studying to show himself approved unto God. Without even knowing it, he communicated to us this priority. So in my devotions, I, too, mark the date and time that I read portions of the Word. Prayerfully, my child will begin to do the same and so on… and so on…

Perhaps the greatest evidence of my parents' roots in our lives is our memorization of scripture. My parents routinely quoted scripture in our presence. During communion each first Sunday for as long as I can remember, my father would quote scripture from memory as communion was served. He not only quoted numerous verses, he connected them for relevancy and sequence. My siblings and I sat through decades of this scripture recitation. If children can learn the lyrics to songs after a few rounds, imagine how many scripture verses we learned by listening to him recite the Word twelve months per year, for five decades! Shame on us if the Word is not hidden in our hearts.

By age five, each of us could recite the church covenant, the Lord's Prayer, the Twenty-third Psalm, Psalm 1, much of Proverbs, and a significant number of salvation verses in the New Testament. We weren't geniuses by any stretch. We were just constantly exposed to the Word. My mother would use scripture verses instead of profanity whenever she was perturbed (I haven't quite grasped this practice). Instead of giving us fair minimum wage for our chores, they gave us a quarter each time we learned a chapter of the Bible. *Hey, a kid's gotta make a living.* We were inundated with the Word of God. So we memorized it. We learned it. And more important, we recalled it in our times of need. We recalled that, When the enemy comes in like a flood, the Spirit of God will raise up a standard against it (Isaiah 59:19b, KJV). And that, There is therefore now no condemnation to them that are in Christ Jesus (Romans 8:1, KJV). And that Greater is he that is in [me] than he that is in the world (1 John 4:4b, KJV). That's what training up children in a Godly manner is all about. It's equipping them with the biblical tools that they'll need to repent, accept, live, endure, and serve. It's teaching them how to seek the will of the Father, and to glorify him in their lives. It's reassuring them that the Lord is their help and strength; that they are safe in his arms. It's giving them a foundation upon which to grow in grace and in the saving knowledge of our Lord Jesus Christ. We give our children everything else that their hearts desire. Why won't we give them what they need the most:a foundation on the Word of God!

Favor

When God gives you a ministry assignment, and you serve him faithfully with all your heart, he grants you favor among men. Such was the case with my father. His impeccable reputation precedes him everywhere. He's been summoned to speak all over the nation, and in every venue. His name is well known, and he's universally respected for his wisdom, biblical knowledge, and clean life. In the early nineties, my father was appointed to the Board of Directors of a reputable Christian university. A few years later, his leadership dexterity, biblical fluency, and lifetime achievements earned him an honorary Doctorate of Divinity degree. I recall the day my family attended his graduation ceremony. It was a monumental event. I was absolutely amazed at the great extent to which the university honored him. I recall how proud we all were of him that day. He was one of only two African-American members of the board of a predominantly Caucasian school, and the only one to be given this recognition. I recall observing him in his doctorate garb and listening to him give his speech. I began to reflect over his life, I realized that this accolade didn't begin to tell the whole story of his attainment, nor did it adequately reflect how truly accomplished he is as a pastor and a man of God. It didn't tell the story of how far the Lord had brought him: from the behaviorally challenged boy in Studguard, Arkansas, to the celebrated Marine, to the seminary student, to the husband, to the Christian leader, to the well-revered pastor. It didn't reveal that while raising a family of four, he took a ministry from eight members to more than two thousand; from the basement of a house to the beautiful church on the hill; from a congregation of babes in Christ to a congregation that was rooted in knowledge of the Word of God. No gimmicks, no musical gift, no political connections, no prosperity promises. He just preached the Word. In and out of season, throughout his ministry, he just preached and lived the Word of God. And the Lord blessed him. The Lord visited the overflow of blessings upon his wife and children. The Lord kept his promise… we did not depart therefrom. The graduation ceremony was very fitting. But my father's life is truly phenomenal, beyond what any award can measure.

A Heart for the People

In the early years, my father established a sort of live-in office at church where he spent a majority of his time. In addition to the time he spent studying and overseeing the affairs of the church, he spent a substantial amount of time with people. He seemed to enjoy opportunities for one-on-one encounters with folks in the neighborhood. And mind you, this was no suburb. Our church, then, was located on a main street at an eventful intersection. He'd often sit outside on the steps of the church and strike up conversation with people that walked by. It didn't really matter who, if they happened to walk by, he'd acknowledge them, and just talk. The street cleaners, the cemetery workers across the street, the local business owners, the youth coming and going from school, community residents, people that stopped in their cars at the stop sign, people that didn't quite come to a complete stop at the stop sign, and any passersby. He struck up conversations with everyone. My father had a knack for relating to people. It didn't matter who they were, where they were from, what they did for a living, or where they were in their lives. He had an uncanny ability to find common ground, or make them comfortable despite uncommon ground. They knew he was a pastor, but talked to him as if he were their friend from way back. It used to amaze me how comfortable people are in his presence! Now I'm used to it. When I first heard the story of Jesus meeting the woman (the harlot) at the well, I immediately thought to myself, *Daddy would do that*. I can say this with confidence because we actually had such a woman in the neighborhood, and she ended up at our church. Funny story…

This, shall we say, lady-of-the-night, used to live in the area and stop in for various church functions after an initial invitation was extended by my dad. She clearly had a great deal of respect for my father because she would put on a few more layers of clothes and modify her appearance when she came around. She finally started attending our Sunday services now and again. I was only six years old at the time, so I didn't quite grasp her evening occupation. All I knew was she wore really cute shoes and was beautiful. You know, that Barbie kind of beautiful if Barbie was a woman of color with smoker lips. Now mind you, my family spent quite a bit of time at the church during the week, so I encountered her regularly, and I grew to like her a lot. In my mind, she was great. She was a Hispanic woman with waist-length hair; she was very thin, and I'm telling you, she wore the coolest stuff! I was sort of turned off by the effervescence of cigarettes that seemed to always surround her, but she was still really cool. I would look forward to her coming around because she always gave me neat little jewelry trinkets. I'd even sneak and sit with her whenever she came to church. Looking back, the members must have enjoyed countless hours of entertainment at my expense as they observed my attachment to this woman. But who knew? I think my siblings may have tried to clue me in, but hanging with her meant they didn't have to watch me, so my welfare was secondary to their convenience I'm sure.

Anyway, the funniest part of this story is that on the Sunday that I was baptized and fellowshipped into the church, she visited. I was so excited to see her there and convinced that she came just for me! So much so that when it came time to assign prayer partners to the new members, I thought, what better pick for me than her! So when the deacon called my name and was just about to announce my prayer partner, I blurted out her name and pleaded with my father to make them assign me to her. Right there in front of the church, the pastor's six-year-old daughter was requesting that a streetwalker, a grown woman, a nonmember, and to my knowledge, a non-Christian, to be her prayer partner. Everyone fell out laughing-everyone except me. I didn't quite get the joke. Even the woman laughed. My father put his head in his hands, then finally whispered to the deaconess to give me to my mother. My mom signaled for me to come and sit next to her for the remainder of the service. The deacons escorted me off the platform. Mom saved seats next to her for both me and the lovely woman each Sunday thereafter, for a very long time. After church that day the woman hugged me, and I heard her both apologizing to and thanking my mom and dad for not putting her out. I'm not sure what ever became of her, but I imagine that her life was forever changed because of her positive experience with the body of Christ.

A large portion of our congregation was built from my dad's encounters with people in the neighborhood. Pastor constantly planted seeds of salvation that the Lord watered and caused to grow. It was just my father's way. People knew him. They respected him. They loved him. And I admired him for it. I can't begin to fathom the number of people that my father has presented the Gospel to and led to Christ. In latter years he's been criticized for being an evangelistic preacher in a time when people want to hear messages of prosperity and deliverance. He certainly presents the Word of God in its entirety, but I believe that he focuses on the salvation message because we're living in the end times. His mandate, his call, is to preach the gospel of Jesus Christ to everyone who will hear it; to make it plain enough for them to understand it; and to pray that they accept it. There are plenty of churches and pastors who will give the people what the people want. I praise God for a true man of God who will preach the Word of God, in and out of season, without altering or otherwise compromising the message.

Portrait of a Virtuous Woman

He who findeth a wife, findeth a good thing!

When I affectionately use the term 'rumor has it,' I mean that I wasn't alive to see it, but I've heard from pretty reliable sources that it is so. Rumor has it that my mom was once a pistol in her early years of marriage, both in the church and at home. Rumor has it that my mom, once upon a time, freely shared her objections in business meetings that she abrasively voiced her discontentment with actions of various guilds, and that she had no problem countering the deacons' position from time to. Rumor has it that my mom used to be a lot like I am now. Wow! Never saw it, can't confirm it, having difficulty imagining it, but I believe it may have been so. My own personality suggests that I may have been predisposed to such an outspoken and passionate disposition, so we'll assume for argument's sake that it's true. In her defense, she had clearly become more tactful and polished before I was old enough to have enjoyed observing this rough part of her.

During my lifetime, my mother established herself as a very poised, revered and highly favored woman of God.

Contrary to how we prioritize things today, she tiered her roles giving greatest priority to her role as helpmate to my father in the ministry; next, to her support role to my father as a wife; then to her role as a mother; and finally to everyone else. Where I come from, children did *not* run the home. We were considered blessings from God, not idols to be catered to, adorned and worshiped. Mom embraced her responsibilities to us as caretaker, nurturer, educator, and preparer. She believed that the best gift she could give us was an environment conducive to salvation, and the tools needed for us to successfully navigate our way through the Christian life. Everything she did seemed part of a strategic plan to equip us for the next phase of our lives. And that she did. Interestingly, she was something different to each of us. It was as if we were each an only child growing up in a world all our own when it came to her. I'm not sure what all she was to each of my siblings, but to me, she was everything. My bet would be that they feel exactly the same. In my early years, she was my protector. In preteen years, she was my advocate both with my father and with older siblings. In adolescence, she became my cheerleader. She constantly affirmed me, supporting all of my efforts and dreams. By the time I reached adulthood, she had become my advisor and very best friend.

My mother was wholly committed to the success of the ministry, but from a different perspective than my father. His role was to preach and teach the Word. Her role was to build spiritual relationships with the people; to meet the people at their place of need, to connect with them, to share with them on a more personal level, to encourage them in their walk, and to be a liaison for the pastor, my father. After preaching on Sundays, my father always retires to his office for meditation and to wind down. My mother, on the other hand, would position herself at the exit doors so that she could greet each person as they walked by, giving handshakes and hugs, and encouraging their hearts. Her hand was always on the pulse of the ministry, while his sight was always on the Lord. What an awesome team! It's no wonder the ministry thrived.

From my recollection, my mother had only a couple of close friends. All of her personal time was spent with my father. She traveled with him everywhere, and supported all of his speaking engagements-all of them. She assisted with counseling sessions that involved women or youth, and helped him wherever he needed her.

Mom held various leadership positions and support roles in the church. She also taught bible clubs in the community, and served at our local community mission. You might ask, how'd she do all that and raise a family? Priorities. More than she was a homemaker she was a pastor's wife. She was good at delegating around the house (four children, remember?). There was such a thing back then as chores and responsibilities. It's where children are assigned specific duties to help out around the house in exchange for basic provisions such as food, clothing, shelter, privileges, and because the parent said so. I don't know how tired my mom was at the end of a day, but *I* was exhausted.

Mom insisted on family devotion at ungodly hours of the morning. We would gather on their bed while she read the Bible and prayed. We mostly dosed. She was also a stickler on proper English, which included no slang, no profanity, and no smacking of the lips in protest. She would actually wash our mouths out with soap when we slipped up. I'll go to my grave defending a few words that I ate soap for that may not have been nice, but were in the dictionary. That makes them proper English! Over my entire childhood, I probably consumed at few cases of soap. Another reason why I went to law school. Another reason I try to use my nice words as often as possible.

Like my father, Mom practiced what she preached. I personally observed her biting her tongue on many occasions when she disagreed with Dad. I heard her pray for people that had wronged her at church. I watched her skillfully navigate her way through the most delicate situations, and gently resolve the most heated debates. And I watched her smile, all the time. She said smiling helped change her countenance and disposition. I haven't mastered that skill either, but I love her for it.

The most powerful display of my mother's virtue occurred in the most trying of times. At age thirty-six, she was diagnosed with a terminal brain tumor (so they thought) while pregnant with my youngest brother. The attending physician, for whom my younger was named, advised my father that there was a better chance of saving a life if they focused exclusively on either mother or child, and not try to save them both. As multitudes of people gathered at the hospital for prayer and support, they observed my mom smiling. As she was wheeled to the operation room, they heard her singing the old hymn My Father Planned it All.

What tho the day may be weary, and dark the shadows fall;
I know wherever he leadeth, my Father planned it all.

He guides my faltering footsteps, along the weary way
For well he knows the pathway, will lead to brighter days

There may be sunshine tomorrow, shadows may break and flee
T'will be the way he chooses, the Father's plan for me

I'11 sing through the shade and the sunshine
I'11 trust him whatever befalls
I'11 sing for I cannot be silent
My Father Planned It All!

What an amazing testimony! We prayed fervently, continually, all day and night. And God answered. Both my mother and newborn brother survived. The tumor caused paralysis on the right side of her body. After months of therapy and years of healing she regained her mobility and about 70% use of her right limbs. It reminded me how Jacob wrestled all night with the Lord in the Old Testament. When morning came, he impacted and crippled Jacob's leg as a permanent reminder that Jacob had spent time with the Lord, and would be blessed. Similarly, my mom spent time with the Lord that night. She fought a good fight and kept the faith. Similarly, her permanent limp in her right leg served as a reminder to her of his grace, and a reflection to all of his goodness. To God be the glory!

    I share these memories because they're important in understanding how crucial it is that we be a witness, in our homes and in our churches. In a day and age of so many uncertainties, people need to be exposed to the hand of God. They need to see, first hand, what God can and will do in the lives of his people. They need to see our demonstrations of faith, and evidence of his deliverance. They need to know our Savior. We must show them, tell them, and invite them into the fold.

The people of God must know that he has a plan for their lives. Not a rough draft, not an idea, but a specific plan. If we understand this truth, then we'll understand our worth. If we understand our worth, then we'll accept our purpose. If we accept our purpose, then we'll glorify our Lord. If we glorify our Lord, then we've fulfilled our call.

A House Divided Cannot Stand

The Wonder Years

Aside from normal sibling rivalry, adolescent rebellion, and occasional spats, I took great pride in the unity of our household while growing up. The Bible tells us (and my mother constantly reminded us) that, a house divided cannot stand (Luke 11:17b, RSV). In ministry life, a house divided is fatal both for the family, and the church. I would say that we mastered the concept of the united front, especially during storms. It was pretty natural to do so in public since in private, our parents kept us on one accord. I don't mean to imply for one moment that we were ever in full agreement. We had a family full of chiefs with not one Indian, so to speak! We rarely agreed on what should be done, how it should be done, why it should be done, or when. But while a meeting of the minds never really occurred in most cases, we always found a way to express, resolve, and move forward. Most times, we expended so much energy in the course of the argument that resolve came by way of sheer exhaustion. I also believe that, to some extent, my siblings and I must have suffered from what is known today as attention deficit disorder when it came to quarrels; a perfectly good argument would commence, but about half way through, we'd sort of loose focus and move on to the next thing. We were just funny that way. We never had a problem moving on. Since we always had company over, guests would often be privy to our quarrels. All of us are communicators yet none of us listeners. My siblings and I weren't too good at taking turns or respecting the others right to speak. We typically expressed ourselves simultaneously. Each chief's opinion was thought to be more valid that all the others, and it was the absolute duty of each chief to fight to the finish until the others both heard and accepted his/her opinion, or until we forgot our point. I'd imagine that some of our guests were a bit ill at ease during these passionate displays of wisdom. I'd imagine they were even more baffled by our swift reconciliation after each fight. Ultimately, we argued not for the purpose of resolve, but based on our right to express an opinion; our right to be heard; our desire to usurp authority over others; our flawed belief that we held all knowledge; and more than anything, our enjoyment of public speaking. Arguments rarely had to do with our personal convictions, and we rarely, if ever, changed the other's mind. It's just what we did. It was a sort of pasttime, a way of fine-tuning our skills of communication and persuasion, and a way of getting by with a thirteen-inch black and white TV with limited program options. We could have a knockdown, drag out at one fifteen in the afternoon, and go to dinner together by six thirty p.m. It didn't take us that long to feel better, it took us that long to finish! At the end of the day, we were fine. We were family. We were tired.

Cherishing the Memories Because They're Funny!

Disseminating Information

All in all we were normal kids with normal lives in a unique position. We were a family of six that grew up in a three-bedroom house for the majority of our childhood, and our parents made it work. My parents did not believe in sparing the rod at all. For some reason, I got most of my rods while at church. Maybe because that's where we spent the majority of time, or maybe because that's where I had my biggest audience and greatest temptations. It wasn't my actions that always got me in trouble, it was my art of communication... my gift for gab... my dissemination of information, if you will. Okay, I talked a lot. But why that was objectionable I never understood, after all, I got it honestly. So I talked, all the time, both in and out of season. I talked during Sunday school; I talked during Vacation Bible School; I talked during worship services. If they were smart, they would have used my gift constructively and let me teach a class or two, especially since I wasn't usually listening to the teacher anyway. Besides, I was better at capturing the audience than the teacher was. My parents didn't quite see it that way, though.

The most embarrassing moment of my life was in service one Sunday when I was sitting with my peers in the children's choir, socially chatting. The fact is, we were *all* talking, not just me. But as always, I was the one whose parents were watching, so I was the one to get caught. At some point during my dad's sermon, he must have said something quite profound because everything suddenly fell silent. Everything, that is, except me. I apparently missed his deep statement and continued on with my own conversation. All of a sudden I was the only one speaking, and the only voice everyone heard! Now, I'm sure that whatever I was saying was of great importance, but my father didn't think so. Everyone *except me* must have seen him pause from his text and look over my way. Without warning, while I was mid-sentence sharing my own wisdom, I heard my father's stern voice in the microphone saying, Aundria, shut up! A deafening silence fell over the congregation. I froze. I couldn't move. I couldn't breathe. I couldn't feel my legs. I couldn't look to my right or left because I was certain that everyone was staring at me, and they were. So I looked straight ahead, beet red, and gave him my undivided attention. After that experience, I still talked. But *never* while my father was preaching, at least not while he's looking my way!

When we share this memory with my father, he claims to have no recollection. That just goes to show you how life impacts all of us differently. Here I am traumatized by an event that he can't even recall. I suppose it's true that we each perceive life through our own lens, and store only those mental pictures that are most significant to us. This one will forever be stored in my database!

Defending his Honor

My youngest brother probably experienced the least amount of parental discipline. He assumes it was because he was the most obedient. I propose that it was because he was the baby. While I can't remember too much ruckus, I clearly recall the day I stayed after school to try out for cheerleading and didn't tell him to wait for me at the gym. Maybe I forgot, maybe I didn't want to walk home with him, maybe I liked a guy on the basketball team. Can't remember that part. Either way he thought I'd left him, so he began to journey home alone when confronted by would-be bullies. Okay, perhaps bully is a strong label for kindergartners, but it makes the story more interesting. Anyhooo, he was leaving the school parking lot when twin brothers who had been picking on him decided to corner him on the playground. Now, at age five, my brother had not yet mastered his present-day conflict resolution skills. And although he wasn't normally violent and may have otherwise walked away, they took his after school snack from his book bag! He knew it would be hours before mom got home to fix a meal, and had no idea when I'd be home, so he made what he thought was a life or death decision to save his snack! It was two against one, so you'd think his chances of success bleak, but there must be something to the theory that people get an unexplainable burst of adrenalin in a life-threatening (or snack- threatening) crisis. Without thought, he launched into both of them with so much force that they both hit the ground simultaneously, and he began pummeling each one. I came out of the school building just in time to be too late. I saw my brother on top of one twin with his head in a chokehold, while the other twin was scooting away on his buttocks and crying. Let me stop here and clarify that my family and I do not condone fighting, especially since most of us can't fight. But this was a sight to behold! My smaller-than-average, mild mannered, little brother… momma's baby… little junior… was defending his honor. Not out of fear, mind you, but over a cream-filled Twinkie. It was great. So after few more rounds I broke things up. I would have done so sooner, but I was curious to see if the twin could get out of the headlock. He couldn't. From that day on we packed him two snacks, just in case. My brother became a state champion wrestler in high school. Go figure.

The Robbery

It's told to me that we once lived in what some might refer to as the ghetto. It's also told to me that we were what some might refer to as poor. Apparently, poverty was a reality for much of our childhood lives, although this fact somehow escaped my awareness! I'm so grateful to my parents for insulating me from this truth and allowing me to believe that we were middle class frugal people whose kids had a substantial inheritance. God bless them for letting me live this dream. The reality is that we once lived in a pretty rough neighborhood. But people were trusting back then, and did unthinkable things like letting a four-year-old boy and a nine-year-old girl walk to the corner candy/liquor/lottery store. These were none other than my older brother and sister. On one of their excursions when they were just about to purchase their jooggi fruits Lemonheads, Alexander the Grapes, Boston Baked Beans, and ten-for-a-dime Bazooka gum, a gunman came in to rob the place. Now think about it. All that candy in hand, and here you are about to be robbed. I'm sure my sister was fit to be tied! The wife of the storeowner reacted quickly and pulled my sister and brother behind the counter just after gunman entered the store. She snuck them in the back room where they ran downstairs to a dark basement. Now, if you're like me, you're wondering why she didn't go too. I guess with all that inventory to protect, she and her husband thought it worth staying upstairs. The long and short of it was, the place got robbed. The police were called after the gunman ran off. No one was hurt. While giving their statements, it dawned on the storeowners that my brother and sister were still down in the basement! If you ever hear either of them tell the story, they were underground for days, with no lights, no water, and only jooggi fruits to keep their frail bodies alive. The reality is, they were down there for approximately twenty minutes, with more than enough candy rations to tie them over until help came.

Good Food, Fellowship, and House Fires

We had an ever-eventful household growing up: four children with two parents who were heavily involved in ministry. This meant that we were often left to our own devices - and what devices they were! My older sister liked to cook, though she never quite got the hang of it during our childhood years. It wasn't the food, but rather the kitchen fires that were the problem! She had an uncanny ability to catch things on fire while cooking, and she did it all the time. It didn't even have to be flammable. She could set anything aflame! Our local fire department was so accustomed to coming to our house that they finally put us on a neighborhood watch and did periodic drive-bys just to make sure there was no smoke coming from our home. She caught everything on fire from oven mitts to the oven itself. She would even manage to ignite the food. How exactly one leaves a cake in the oven long enough for it to burst into flame was beyond us all, but she accomplished it repeatedly! She meant well, and would actually get through a meal every now and again without incident. For some ungodly reason my parents allowed her to keep practicing-perhaps in hopes that she would fine-tune her skills. That was until the final incident in 1989, when my siblings, my infant daughter, and I had to immediately evacuate the house and run to my aunt's down the street because of a small grease fire that we couldn't quite put out. The kitchen was salvaged, our house was fine, but at that point, my dad purchased a microwave oven.

Dogs, Trouble, and More Dogs

My oldest brother had a true spirit of adventure. Growing up, he had the most experience with the *rod of correction* being applied to the *seat of understanding*. He was a trooper though. He took his lumps, regularly. A typical boy, he explored every danger from jumping off the garage just to see if he could land on his feet, to sticking a hairpin a socket to see if it would really explode. He didn't land on his feet, and the socket did explode. He wore a Michael Jackson glove for three days to conceal the burns from my parents, then finally fessed up when I noticed that his whole hand had turned black and blistery, and he couldn't stop me from crying at the dinner table. Again, we just weren't good at covering stuff up.

His greatest capers involved rescuing dogs that he found on his paper route and hiding them in our basement to keep as pets. Now, we're unsure of where and what these dogs were rescued from, especially since some of them had collars. Nonetheless, eight dogs rescued, eight separate occasions, all named Pepper, all discovered by my dad. Each one was gotten rid of immediately, each one resulted in disciplinary action. Needless to say, my brother didn't always grasp lessons the first time. I recall sitting outside his bedroom door time after time as he got his lickins from my father, crying and pleading with my brother not to do whatever he'd done anymore. After all, my heart couldn't take it!

A Tale of the Princess, the Peacemaker, Politician, and the Prodigal

It's amazing that siblings can be alike in so many respects, yet drastically different in others. We came from the same parents, the same home, the same set of circumstances, yet were somehow nurtured very differently. As a result, we each developed distinctive characteristics that both complimented and clashed on every level. We share gifts such as articulation, humor, perception, vision, charisma, stubbornness, self-centeredness, and assertiveness. But our gifts manifest themselves in very different forms as they're influenced by our unique traits. Allow me to share the characteristics, the persons, of my siblings for the sake of perspective on how each of us navigated our way though the call, and through our lives in ministry, both individually and collectively.

The Princess:

My older sister is probably the most unique and fascinating one of us all. I title her the princess because she is the epitome of a damsel in distress, and was always a Daddy's girl growing up. From changing a light bulb to fueling a gas tank, she just couldn't (or wouldn't) do it. She's always lived a sort of charmed life that you can't help but envy. The neat part is that she's neither incompetent nor passive, just privileged. She has a stunning gift of subtle coercion, an ability to enlist support and gain compliance from others. She's great at surrounding herself with those who accommodate her selective handicaps, and help her accomplish whatever the task. Her peers played into it. I played into it. My brothers played into it, but most of all, my father was her knight. He's a caretaker by nature and believes wholeheartedly that taking care of women is an inherent responsibility of manhood. I love that about him. He accommodated my sister to an almost ridiculous extent. But then who didn't! She seems to always land at the center and has a real knack for causing others to sort of orbit around her world. You'd have to see it to believe it, but trust me when I tell you, it's amazing! One can't help but envy such a gift, and it was just that, a true gift. One that most of us would give anything to have.

My sister has always been highly connected to, and committed to, ministry. She assumed leadership roles very early. While the rest of us established interests outside of the church, my sister's sole comfort zone *was* the church. With the exception of high school gospel choir, she had no use for extracurriculars apart from the ministry. All that she did, all that she was, was somehow connected to our church. And she acclimated well to this environment. We differed greatly in this respect. Because of our eight-year age gap, it wasn't until early adulthood that my sister and I connected at all. But when we did so, we did so completely. I thank God for her; for the things that she taught me both directly and indirectly; for her paving the way for me in so many respects; for her assistance early on with my child, and for being a part of my transition into adulthood. Most of all, I'm thankful for how she subconsciously groomed me for ministry.

Despite her princess role of convenience, her role in ministry, and in the family, was the pseudo-leader. She was the one we looked to both as the oldest, and as the most connected. She always had a plan, a project, a vision. And with a strong will, a passionate conviction, and a tough exterior, she most often met success. Over the years, my sister was extremely hard on me. That turned out to be a blessing. She inadvertently taught me the importance of understanding who we are, of accepting our role of leadership, and of becoming immune to the voices of ridicule, discouragement, and defeat. These lessons became critical to survival and success in ministry. She ultimately helped me learn to insulate myself from the snares of the outside world, and the church, especially after the birth of my child. For that, I will always love her dearly. In spite of all, I wouldn't trade one aspect of our relationship, nor would I ever change her. I thank God for her existence in my life. I thank God for the princess.

The Peacemaker:

This is my eldest brother. He is very intelligent, yet has a heart of gold. What a rare combination. My brother has always desired harmony. He's highly functional in harmonious climates, and almost incapacitated in any other. He, too, has an awesome ability to attract people. He has a subtle charisma and is the ultimate gentleman. He's quite a bit more discriminating than my sister with whom he allows in his inner circle. Being at the center is not quite as pertinent for him. As I recall, he has always kept his personal world a bit more private than the rest of us. But he's a people-person all the same. He's the kind of person that you have to work hard not to like, and he'd have to work even harder not to like you. This came in handy for me during my schooldays as I fed off of his reputation and sailed through on a flowery bed of ease as his little sister. It was my brother that made me want to be in a band. He started a band in high school and played the bass guitar. I, too, learned to play bass guitar with hopes of getting in. They let me where the jacket and carry their instruments, but that was the extent of it. To this day, I'm determined to join the band! Never mind that I've forgotten how to play the instruments.

Although he would never admit it, he is highly sensitive. He's sensitive to his own pain, and to that of others. I would share with you that the nickname my dad used to call him growing up was 'teardrop' because of his sensitivity, but that would be embarrassing to both of them so I'll keep that detail to myself. Besides, he's grown out of the teary phase.

He privately processes his emotions, but they are apparent all the same. I love this part of him. It makes him easy to talk to, easy to connect with, and easy to be around. He strives to create harmony in the most unharmonious situations and seems to dedicate himself to bringing everyone on one accord. My brother is an eternal optimist. Anything is possible. Nothing is insurmountable. All can be accomplished if one's attitude is positive enough to work through the storm. This makes him an excellent leader, a great motivational speaker, and an exceptional man.

In childhood, my older brother was always a dreamer. He would dream so much, and so big, that those of us around him couldn't help becoming believers. He always thought in dynamic terms. And he always found himself looking forward to the next dream. We have this in common. We also have in common a spirit of restlessness that keeps us constantly moving toward the next level, the next ideal, the next day.

In the worst of times, you need dreamers. In the worst of times, particularly in more recent times, my brother served as our mediator, our optimist, our motivator, our dreamer. He desires to be the glue that keeps us all bonded together, and he's effective at making us want to stay bonded. I grieved for months when he left for college. We were pretty connected most of our lives, and I missed him dearly. I couldn't wait until sibling weekends so I could go down to visit him at Ohio State to be the little sister all over again.

We all thought he would become a minister someday because he has such a spirit of encouragement. Instead, he uses this gift in the secular world, and is probably more effective therein. He's a lifeline, without even knowing it. Even now, he gives me perspective, hope, and a sense of peace in the midst of troubling times. He inherited my father's supreme leadership skills. The best leaders know how to serve. They are both servants, and they are both effective leaders. He was the constant of us all, the steady hand, the one that made things a little funnier and a little easier. I loved him dearly growing up. I love him more now. *Teardrop* has come a long way, God bless him!

The Politician:

If I speak of my youngest brother with favor, it's because a part of me favors him. Not that I love him more, but in a different way. I was five years old when he was born, and my mom was in the early stages of rehabilitation and recovery after her brain tumor. He was our *miracle child*, he and my mom survived labor only by the grace of God. Because my mom was still wheelchair bound, my grandmother moved in temporarily to help care for my infant brother and provide general supervision. This meant that the rest of us had to become independent and fend for ourselves in many respects. As we got older, I voluntarily took on a sort of surrogate role with my younger brother, and in my mind, he was my child. In my mind, he still is. In his mind, he'd like me to get over it. Good luck with that!

My younger brother has been a natural politician his whole life. He has had a platform of one sort or another since I can remember. Unlike the rest of us, he typically has an actual position in a debate. Hence, he's much more passionate of a debater. In elementary school, he would engage kids on the playground on various topics, and impress upon them the importance of standing up for what they believed. Whether the issue was chocolate milk at lunchtime or racial equality, he was the advocate for justice. He was so adamant on the human rights and equality issue that he befriended the Caucasian twins that he'd beaten up only days before so that the playground could return to its normal state of chaotic amity. Since then, he's made a point to create an extremely diverse personal world where the only criterion for admission is that you have an opinion of your own, and are willing to consider his.

Years ago my baby brother' had an opportunity to travel to Ghana, West Africa on a mission trip sponsored by our church. This trip changed his life forever. I recall him coming back determined to evoke change in our schools, our communities, our churches, and our homes. In Africa, he encountered youth who craved education, revered adults, and were rooted in family values. He encountered a culture that was grateful for their very existence, let alone anything and everything else they were blessed to acquire. He encountered youth who were taught to be the best they could be simply for the sake of humanity rather than for economic gain. Wow. Needless to say, that when he returned to the States he was less than content with our way of life, and was compelled to affect change. Improvement of humanity became his new platform. It still is.

Only recently did my family and I realize how many lives my younger brother has impacted, and how deep an impression he's left on so many. He has friends and colleagues all over the county — even outside of the United States – who not only hold him in high esteem, but who he connects with regularly. Through him we've met folks from literally all over the world, and in all walks of life. The more we learn of his world, the more we're impressed by his person.

The most unique thing about my younger brother is that he defines himself, and his success, based upon the extent to which he positively impacts others. It matters to him that others leave his presence with a compelling impression, whether positive or negative, one that stimulates progress. He is highly intelligent (obnoxiously so), and surrounds himself with people who sharpen his intellect. He has a heart for his fellow man, a heart for excellence, and a heart for evolution from indifference and stagnation to conviction and achievement. There's an old saying, if you don't stand for something, you'll fall for anything. He won't likely fall for much, because the foundation he stands on is so strong.

Having said all of that, we still enjoyed many hours of entertainment at his expense as he found his way growing up. He was always a what if kid: What if I could dig a hole far enough in the ground to actually reach another continent? He tried it. He dug up an army of ants and had to be carried inside to the bathtub in garbage bags. What if I spray curl activator on my lips, will they, too, curl up? He tried it. They did, sort of. His lips swelled to the size of oranges, and he couldn't talk for several days. What if I don't comb my hair for a month? Will it grow faster and dred on its own? We'll never know the answer to this one. My dad took him to the barber and had his head shaved low as a lesson in grooming and hygiene ... just in time for church the following Sunday. What if I run for office in a ward that is desperate for change and could benefit from my input, even though I have no campaign funding and the incumbent has held office for decades? He tried it, and shook the very foundation of our city. Even without winning, he was victorious at leaving a permanent impression that has paved the way for positive change and left his mark on society. He's amazing.

I had the pleasure of watching him grow through every phase of his life. From walking him to class on his first day of kindergarten to attending his championship wrestling matches in high school, I observed his transformation from infancy to manhood. While I'd like to take credit for all that he is, he is my mother's child. His value system is that of my mom; his passion comes from my mom; his integrity comes from my mom; his legacy-orientation comes from my mom. Her imprint on his life is distinct. I simply had the privilege of watching the impression as it was made, and gleaming gems from the process. His life was intentionally preserved by God in my mother's womb, and the Lord saved both their lives to complete a great work through each one. He is a living, breathing testimony, and the most paramount evidence of my mother's faith in God. She was, and remains, his foremost influence. I praise God for that.

As the critical thinker, he is the perspective of the situation. As the strongest heart, he disseminated courage to us all. But when all is said and done, he's still my baby brother. And I'll always love him as just that.

The Prodical:

Unlike the Bible story I didn't forsake my family, demand my inheritance in advance, squander it on libations and liberties then return for love and shelter when all other options were exhausted. Although I would welcome any inheritance at any time (cause I have a soft place in my heart for really nice stuff), I'm nothing like the prodical son in the Bible. But given my tendency to speak freely, question tradition, live a more normal life than what the church was ready to tolerate, and generally be who I was, the *prodical daughter* title was assigned to me very early in life. So I went with it. The next two chapters will offer more detail both on how I obtained this title and to what extent it was fulfilled. It suffices to say for now that the title speaks more about distinctions between myself and my siblings than about who I really am.

Perhaps the most distinctive aspects of my nature growing up were self-expression, imagination, and caretaking. Like my siblings, I was born with an Alpha personality and no problem expressing my thoughts, opinions and positions despite opposition. Everyone wanted to be part of my quad on the school debate team. And even when my side lost Moot Court sessions in college (which was rare), we always had the most impressive dialogue. Imagination breeds vision, and vision (nurtured) breeds action. My imagination is vivid. I don't see dead people. I don't talk to invisible friends, but I have a knack for seeing far beyond what exist right now, into the possibility of what *could* exist. A wise person said that, vision without action is just imagination. So, I pride myself as a risk-taker who transforms her imaginations into vision, and her vision into action. Success is not always the end result, but I'm rarely left wondering what if. I usually know what if, because for better or worse, I usually take the risk to find out!

In our family, I'm the caretaker: the one who handles the problem, bears the weight of the world on her shoulders (necessarily or not), manages crisis, fixes stuff. In my mind, every problem has a solution, every mission can be accomplished, every upset is temporary. I, too, am an eternal optimist-even in the most pessimistic circumstances. I guess this was my contribution. It's the only way I know how to survive.

Strength in Unity

With all of these alpha personalities, it's hard to imagine that we could accomplish even the remotest sense of cohesion, let alone unity! The unifying link was my parents. Thank the Lord for unity in my parents' marriage, in their commitment to raising their children in the fear and admonition of the Lord, and in their walk with the Lord. They didn't just teach the Word, they lived it. If my mother never held a family devotion, her life would have shown us how to live. If my father never preached a sermon, his character taught us how to behave. They aren't just good Christian role models, they are godly examples of what a mother and father should be. They didn't have to lecture us a lot. They exemplified the standard, and demonstrated enough love to make us want to meet the standard set. Before we ever understood our charge to please God, we desired to please them. We wanted to make them proud. We wanted to reap what they had sown, we wanted our lives to be like theirs. Even today, we desire to honor their legacies.

Unity helped us stay grounded. Unity kept us focused. Unity kept us strong. Unity enabled us to survive. God has shown my family tremendous favor. Despite our periods of arrogance, rebellion, disobedience, and lack of submission to his will, he never let us step outside the realm where his love could reach and bless us. At times, we strayed, but we never departed. As promised in his Word, he began a work that he is performing until the day of redemption. He graciously glorified himself in our lives. I often asked my parents why they thought he chose our family. Why us? They never knew, nor do I. But we're ever thankful that he did. It has been an absolute privilege to take part in the building of his kingdom. It is an honor to be called his own.

Please know that there are times when life in ministry will threaten, and even tear, the very fabric of a family unit, no matter how strong or unified it is. There are circumstances that will, in fact, divide a house. Stress from the church, stress from the standard, stress from weight of bearing others' burdens along with your own, and stress from the sense of helplessness that you're not making an impact or accomplishing your God-given call. These stresses and others can cause dissension in the ranks. There were times when it absolutely did! In recent years, our family has unwittingly tested the theory of the divided house, and we are now painfully aware that it, indeed, will not stand. I'll share more of this test in later chapters. It suffices for now to say that our Savior's grace is bigger than our sins, and his mercy is more bountiful than our shortcomings. Praise God.

Whatever house you're apart of: be it family, church, ministry work, whatever it may be, know that the key to overcoming adversity is unity. Division within leads to deterioration without. No family or ministry will last amidst segregation. We must become one in the Spirit, and one in our purpose. We must unite in our cause of pleasing Christ, and fulfilling his commission on our lives. God bless you as you move forward, together.

The Separation Sacrifice

From the outside looking in, the first family seems a coveted existence. If you, too, watched the 2008 presidential election, you may have done so with a certain amount of envy. What a couple, what a family, what a life! But consider the separation sacrifice. The sacrifice of being separated from personal, intimate, meaningful relationships and fellowship with people with whom you have a desire to be with, and who have a genuine desire to be with you. Consider a life wherein you are constantly surrounded by people, always at the center, invited to every function-not because of your person, but because of what your person represents: not because of *who* you are, but rather *what* you are: not because of what others desire to do for you, but because of what they perceive that you can do for them. Being a part of a first family on a substantially smaller scale, I wouldn't wish their position on anyone. God bless them for accepting the challenge.

Public life forces a private separation because you don't always have the luxury of choosing your associations. You're expected to be emotionally neutral; to interact with everyone the same, regardless of religion, race, color, creed, or whether or not you even *like* them. If preference is shown for any, the others cry *its favoritism, its discrimination,* or, to coin a church phrase, *it's a click.* A click, by the way, is a small nucleus of people who opt to spend time together and open their worlds to one another because they have some common ground, or simply enjoy each other's company. Now, it kind of sounds to me like the common art of human relationship building. But when you're the first family, you're not allowed to participate in common human behaviors. Thus, the practice of selecting your preferred company is identified as inappropriate formation of *clicks.* Go figure.

On the surface the idea of being on every guest list might seem great. We were never alone on holidays or special occasions. We always had a place to go, a place to be, something to do, a reason to exist. Given this scenario, how in the world could I ever convince an onlooker how emotionally separated we actually were, and how desperately lonely life often was. I longed for true friendship; for genuine connections to other human beings with no strings, no demands, no ulterior motives, no standards, and no requirements attached. I used to look around the church and pick out individuals that I might like to trade places with. I focused on people who were very reserved, and who sort of faded into the background, almost invisible. I used to imagine their lives; wondering what kind of person they were, what types of things they liked to do, and who the significant people were in their lives. I imagined them living their day to day, and envied them for their aura of privacy. Mostly, I envied them their opportunity to be accepted, loved, and connected just based upon who they were and not for the position they held. I wasn't crazy or anything, I just had no concept of what such a life could possibly be.

The reality is, even if we were offered a normal, faceless existence, we probably wouldn't function very well therein. Growing up, there were certainly times when my siblings and I enjoyed being the center of attention. Each one of us inherited a level of charisma that afforded us contact with people from various walks of life. One of the skills we developed as first kids was manipulating environments in our favor, both in and outside of the church. We were also uninhibited communicators, so we found it easy to strike up conversation with anyone. We never met a stranger, and could find common ground with just about everyone. We inherited this trait from my father. Most significantly, we were the pastor's kids! That in and of itself commanded a certain amount of respect from others, even those who didn't like us at all. We often capitalized on my father's achieved reverence in the church and in the community, and were benefactors of his positive reputation. By most standards we were pretty decent kids. We desired to please our parents, and for the most part, we were careful not to undermine my father's position. The family name was import to us, and we worked hard to protect it. This meant that we couldn't do all the things that other kids did; we couldn't attend all the events that others attended; and some crowds, activities, and basic youth stuff were off limits to us. Stop the violins though, most of the time this was a pretty fair trade off for the fringe benefits on the other side of the coin.

The harder sacrifices came later on when we were old enough and mature enough to realize that out of the hundreds of people in our social sector, we struggled to name one or two whom we believed had our best interest at heart. We learned that we couldn't fully trust friendships or romance in the church setting, because there was so great an opportunity for us to be used, misled, or otherwise compromised. Eventually, we accepted the necessity of living in a sort-of bubble, and began to establish an island of our own. We managed to build a discriminating little fortress around ourselves. We never stepped outside of our fortress for any reason. Others came into our world, we rarely went into theirs. We stayed emotionally tucked away in private, while putting ourselves on the front line in public. Our house was the hangout. Our world was the social setting. We were only truly ourselves at home. Looking back it was sort-of fascinating. We acted as if we weren't allowed to go outside and play; we could only have company come in and see us. We always stayed in our own comfort zone. That's how it was, all the time, all our lives. Kind of crazy, but I don't think any of us saw our situation as odd or problematic. After all, it offered a kind of security, an insulation from the harshest parts of ministry life. And it worked quite well in former years when the family was fully intact and relational needs were simple. As we entered adulthood and found ourselves still semi-disconnected from the world, I slowly began to realize how our years of separation now made it quite challenging to exist in normal realities and conduct healthy, meaningful relationships. I'm not sure we even considered the extent to which we crutched one another, and were co-dependent on our family unit, that is, until the family unit was broken. Only then did we reluctantly migrate to our own worlds and begin the process of finding our own way. That, too, was dreadful.

It's unfortunate that ministry life often promotes isolation instead of integration, and practices love at a distance. Understandably, some degree of isolation is necessary in any public existence. After all, fully connecting to our environment and all of the individuals therein would not only be impossible, but would be absolutely exhausting. As we work to establish acceptable boundaries though, we often err on the side of widening the gap between ourselves and others a little too far. In an effort to maintain appropriate relationships, we tend to deny ourselves the benefit of others. And deny others the benefit of the *real* us. We hesitate to share our problems or cry on another's shoulder for fear of compromising our position or becoming too transparent. There's that word again. It's even more probable that we fail to make such connections simply because we never learned how.

My parents were married for forty-two years. They traveled together. They worked together. They played together. They ministered together. They made decisions together. They vacationed together. They confided in one another. They did everything with each other. I know that my mom had women with whom she associated from time to time, and my dad would interact with other pastors and pool-shooting buddies now and again. But they seemed to be with one another almost 100 percent of the time. They were true soul mates, confidantes. Their innermost secrets were shared with one another. Their most precious time was spent with one another. They had a genuine love for people, and dedicated their lives to meeting the spiritual and practical needs of others. But their private world was theirs alone, shared with no one else. Looking back, it almost seems strange. Who would want to spend every waking moment with their spouse? What about shopping and lunch with the girls, or fishing with the guys? What about girl gossip and boy bragging? What about Monday night football and Saturday super-sales? What about *just get away from me for a while and give me some space*! But that wasn't their sentiment, at least not that I witnessed. He was the pastor. He had a congregation, but no close friends. She was a first lady. She had people she ministered to, but not girlfriends to serve as venting outlets. I'm sure that they made occasional phone calls. And I know for a fact that my mom had at least two dear friends that honor the memory of their friendship even today. But the overall theme of their marriage and ministry seemed to be a sacrifice of separation. They kept themselves apart, isolated, and protected for untainted, unadulterated use by God.

Again, children learn what they live. So, the rest of our family followed suit. As teens, we couldn't rationalize the reasons why we were so discriminating with our environments and protective of our interactions, but we were. We'd subconsciously learned separation. We embraced it. We made peace with it. We, to some extent, celebrated it. Now with each of us in our third or fourth decade of life, change seems unlikely. We can learn to let others in, but I doubt that we'll ever be able to fully connect. Thank God, for our spouses, and for those who've always stood in the gap whether we wanted them to or not. Thank God, for those that he brought into our lives to help fill the tremendous void left after the recent disruption in our family unit. Thank God, that despite our own disconnectedness, we were always able to connect to and fellowship with him.

While my siblings and I had a built-in support system, my daughter didn't have it so easy. As an only child, she wasn't privy to such support. Yet, her experiences with separation in the ministry were exactly the same: same isolation, same challenges, same bubble, same glass house. A couple of years before leaving for college, she was alienated from her church peer group over disagreements that started small, but left unchecked by leadership, escalated to a point of no return. She was alienated from the majority of her church peers in the process, and opted out of the respective youth ministries. Disheartened and disillusioned by church altogether, she, too, began to seek other outlets. Despite being one generation removed, she was still part of the first family. Consequently, *who she was* took precedence over *how she felt*. What others thought *she* should do as the pastor's granddaughter took precedence over what had been done to her. And while she exemplified the precise behaviors of all of the other youth involved, her standard was higher, her consequence was greater, and her reputation was most harmed, and for her (and her alone) these behaviors were deemed unacceptable.

She was groomed enough to know her actions would not go unpunished, and she took her lumps well. But what hurt her the most was that none of the others involved suffered any repercussions at all, nor were they required to take any responsibility for the events and outcomes. Yet, she's the pastor's granddaughter-my daughter. It didn't matter that she was only sixteen and the youngest of all involved, there was a prescribed formula for how she should behave, respond, and resolve conflict. There was a greater expectation of her conduct. She was the one that would have to step down from ministry. She was the one that would be shunned by her peers in the negative aftermath. She was the one who had to find a way to regain, and maintain integrity. She was the one who had to apologize and seek resolve. I insisted on it. It's what I knew. It's what I taught. It's what she half-heartedly understood, but it's what she did. My child never mastered all of the charismatic techniques that the rest of us so easily employed. She shot from the hip and was much more genuine with her emotions. Now, here she was with a broken heart and damaged reputation-not from the world, but at the center of ministry. Wow. My next statement will seem harsh and insensitive but here it is: all of this goes with the territory. Our choices in these instances are limited. It's not about us. It's about the body of Christ and the kingdom of God. We can *defend ourselves*, or we can *preserve our testimony*. Our most extreme hardships have turned out for the greater good, and so we suck it up, and we press on.

This whole experience made both my daughter and I realize that it was time for her to find her own voice. I didn't want her to spend the rest of her life focusing more on the expectations of others than on obedience to God. I wanted her to begin establishing her own personal relationship with Christ. I wanted her to know who she is much early on than I, and identify her unique purpose in the kingdom. Unlike the rest of us, I wanted her to be shaped solely by Christ, not by ministry. It wasn't necessary for her to get bruised, battered, and bitter like the rest of us, this wasn't her call. I believe with all my heart that God has a very different plan for her life, and my prayer is that she'll be far enough away from the madness of our world to hear him when he calls, and close enough to him to answer.

Now away in college, she's learning her person, and finding her way. She has a new voice now, and it sounds great! Neither she nor I had any idea how difficult our separation from one another would be, or how strange it would be for her to function in a new world. But she's trained up in the way she should go, and I'm believing God that the same grounding that empowered me will keep establish her footing and equip her for spiritual success. I am confident that the same God the kept me will keep her. Prayerfully, the Lord will ultimately lead her to a new church home, make room for her gifts, and allow her to exercise them according to his plan for her life.

Here's the rainbow. During the most difficult times in our lives, we had very few options for comfort, which means that we had no other choice but to depend on Jesus Christ. Each of us has been forced to rely upon our relationship with the Lord to guide us through life's most trying moments. He's been my advisor, my supporter, my motivator, my affirmation, my comfort, my peace. Dad taught us that in the absence of friends, the Lord would be the friend that sticketh closer than a brother (Proverbs 18:24, KJV). He has been, and for this, I rejoice.

As you experience periods of isolation, loneliness and separate in your own life, I encourage you, too, to rely upon Christ as the only constant that you may ever have. While God is gracious enough to give us other fulfilling connections in the forms of spouses, children, friends, family members, church members, co-workers, and spiritual leaders, he never intends for these to be our primary relationships. The Bible says that God is a jealous God, and he commands us to have no other gods before him. That means that nothing and no one else should take priority over our relationship with him. He desires us to get to know him intimately, and to have continual fellowship with him. Others can often be a distraction to private time with Christ. I've learned the hard way of his desire for our undivided attention, and our wholehearted submission to him. When my life of separation via ministry was not sufficient to get me closer to him, he began removing those in my inner circle. I don't know for certain that all of these losses were for the purpose of bringing me closer to Christ. But I do know that my fellowship with my Savior has been an invaluable outcome.

Under the Spotlight

> To the families and individuals that I've interviewed and/or had the pleasure of knowing, who have opted out of the spotlight and left church ministry because of the overwhelming cost, my heart goes out to you. I can imagine the casualties that you must have suffered in your line of duty; and my prayers will continue for your healing, reconciliation, and peace.

Someone once said that the curse of a great leader is that he makes it look so easy that everyone under him thinks they can do his job. Okay, maybe I just made that up, but it's true all the same. If you're a great pastor, the associate ministers and deacons begin to think, *I can do that*. If you're a skilled choir director, the choir members tend to think, *I could do that*. Or, *why doesn't she do it like this?* Bleacher fans always think they could throw better, catch better, dunk better, and T-off better than the pro. Every spectator seems to know better than the player how to win the game. Every subordinate seems to know better than the leader what should be done. After all, you don't have to actually play the game to know how, right? And just because you've never done it, and never demonstrated the competence to do it, doesn't mean that you can't.

Well, aside from the very relevant issue of competence, the more pressing issue is that sideliners are not under the spotlight. They're not in the pressure of the game. They don't have full perspective, and they're not operating with full information. Often times they know just enough to be ill-informed, and observe just enough to draw a wrong conclusion. The warped mind-set seems to be *if only the leaders do this, if only the key players do that, if only those in charge would operate for the benefit of the majority, the spectators, the naysayers, the observers, the sidelines, the critics, the fare-weather fans (and members, and friends), then all would be well.* Even as kids we used to say if I were king, I would... then follow the statement with some far-fetched, ridiculous decree that we would set in place to make the world, specifically *our* world, a better place. Our input seemed quite reasonable, at least from the outside looking in. But why doesn't anyone ever consider the view from the inside, looking out?

Church leaders are frequently victims of such short-sighted scrutiny. It rarely occurs to the congregation that the man of God likely operates from a full-view lens. In most cases, he has more information, carries more experience, and considers things from a greater perspective than the members and subordinate leaders. Yet, this often earns him very little trust where the conflicting opinions of others are involved.

As choir director for one of our largest music ministries, I've experienced sideline critics over and over again. Inside looking out, it translates something like this:

Why choose that song? Why wear that uniform? Why minister at that service, or for that occasion? Why stop rehearsal to address that issue? Why include Bible Study or prayer during rehearsal—we're here to learn songs? What gives her the right to make that rule? Why do we have to do that? Why is everything about our spiritual growth? Why is she in such a bad mood today? Why didn't she speak to me? Why isn't she close to the members? Our choir would be better if she were more approachable. Our choir would be bigger if she were less approachable. She needs to be stricter. She has too many rules. We need to sing more fast stuff. We need to sing more slow stuff. She can't dictate the service, who does she think she is? Why doesn't she have more input in the service, isn't that her job?

And the scrutiny goes on, and on, and on. If you do well, you're arrogant. If you fail, you're incompetent. If you strive to keep peace, you're weak. If you stand firm and minimize democracy, you're a dictator. If you wear black, you're morbid. If you wear red, you're pagan. If your hair is short, you're masculine. If your hair is long, you're fake. If you're thin, you're conceited. If you're fat, you're offensive. If you wear sweats, you're unkept. If you wear heels, you're over the top. If you reach out to one, you're showing favoritism. If you reach out to none, you're distant and have no love for people. If you reach out to all, you're drained, ineffective, and soon to be disillusioned! *If I were king, I would*... and the list goes on.

To leaders who find themselves in these situations, stop looking out and look up. People don't have the answers, unless they hear a word from the Lord. My personal advice would be to go directly to the Source, as third party information can often get misconstrued in the delivery process. If the Lord does in fact speak thru someone else to minister to you, he will, no doubt, prepare your heart to receive the message, and will create a proper atmosphere for delivery. He does all things well.

At the point that God gives us a specific directive, we simply cannot afford to be distracted by the opinions and agendas of others. We have a charge to keep, a work to perform, a Savior to glorify. We must love, and show love toward, our brothers and sisters in Christ, but cannot allow them to compromise our obedience and good standing with our Lord.

Under the spotlight, everything that we say, do, and are will be scrutinized. That is the unwavering reality. Our challenge is to make sure that the voice that we hear and respond to is the Lord's, and that through his eyes, and from his perspective alone, we view our ministry and our lives.

Preacher's Kids

I'm sure you've heard the popular expression preacher's kid or PK, probably in a derogatory tone, with the follow-up comment that *those are the worst ones*. Interestingly enough, people have made this remark since what seems like the dawn of time. They say it right in our presence, all the time. Just a note to the masses, if we're in the room, we can hear you! Even as young children we're savvy enough to determine that this is a derogatory reference to us. At any rate, this is a common stereotype that many hold, and that our church families have conditioned the masses to believe.

It's no wonder that many children of pastors and other public figures break under the pressure of the spotlight. In fairness, there are those of us who really do act out beyond the norm, sometimes because we simply live up to the negative expectations of others, and other times we simply rebel against a standard that we perceive to be excessively high. But at the end of the day, please consider the most reasonable explanation for our behaviors ... we're *human*! Like everyone else, we navigate our way through childhood, adolescence, and young adulthood listening to a number of voices: our parents, our peers, society, and, let's face it, our own sinful nature. Like others, we make poor choices at the worst of times. Yet, we're caught under the perpetual spotlight for all the world to see. In these circumstances, the gossip mills operate in full force; our reputations are often irreversibly damaged; our embarrassment is compounded by the public awareness of our screw-up; our self-esteem is severely compromised; and worst of all, the *preacher's kid* myth is perpetuated.

Certainly it's normal for people to attack and gossip rather than uplift and support, that's just human nature. It's just a little more hurtful when it happens within the confines and protections of your church home. And it's a lot more detrimental when it happens to children. The outcome is often a complete disconnection from the body of Christ, or at least, a tainted view of ministry. Yet, many of us have no choice but to stay right there in ministry's midst. We still have to serve and protect. We still have to meet the relentless standard. We still have to get back on the front line. We were bruised, damaged, heartbroken, angry, and completely disillusioned.

It is because of such situations in my own life that I had varying feelings throughout my youth about the church body, and being a pastor's daughter. Let me say that I fully accept the notion that *to whom much is given, much is required*. So, I don't mean to imply for one moment that we should not have a higher standard than others, or that we should not be taught and mandated to live exemplary lives. We absolutely have a responsibility to positively represent our parents, our church, our Lord, and the kingdom of God! We are the first ones people see when they come to Worship. We're often the first impression, the initial point of contact, the make-or-break variable. Hence, we understandably have very little room for error when souls are potentially at stake. Yet and still, maturity comes with age, time, and experience. As children, we have benefit of none of the above. As teens, we're still learning our role. As young adults, we're dealing with the aftermath of all the times we got it wrong. And believe me, all of us will at some point get it wrong. So despite the standard, despite the requirement, despite the souls that are at stake, the waters sometimes get too rough for us to tread, the forest is often too thick to navigate through, and we simply loose our way.

The Prodigal Daughter

Allow me to become completely transparent for a few moments. What I share next is not for my own release- praise God that he's already freed me. It's rather to give you an up close and personal look at what life is truly like under the spotlight, when you're young, transitioning through the various stages of life, and haven't quite gotten your sure footing. Again, God has been gracious in bringing me out, but the following paragraphs depict the place where I spent a large majority of my life.

Earlier I mentioned the softer, less controversial aspects of being deemed a prodigal. In most respects, though, the connotation was absolutely objectionable. Perhaps by default, perhaps by design, perhaps through self-fulfilling prophecy, perhaps for my future testimony's sake, I used to be known throughout our church environment as our family's prodigal daughter. Unlike the bible story, I wasn't old enough to have asked dad for my inheritance to run off and sew my oats, but perhaps I displayed characteristics that indicated that I someday would, I don't know. For decades, I carried the negative implications of a title spoken into existence by others in the church. They spoke negative prophecy into my life so frequently, and so consistently, that I came dangerously close to fulfilling their discouraging predictions. Thank God that not all prophecy is prophetic. Thank God that his voice rang louder, and truer, then theirs. Only recently have I begun to see myself through God's eyes and stop defining who I am based on world view. Believe me, it's a process.

Anyway, they called me the prodigal child for as long as I can remember. It was initially started by the lovely members of our extended family who were also members of our congregation when I was very young-too young to exhibit any prodigal behaviors or to even begin to rebel. But the combination of me being my mother's most difficult pregnancy, having an early mind of my own, and not being quite as fond of them as the rest of my siblings were somehow deemed me to be a problem. In fairness, I did sort of dance to the beat of my own drum growing up, and apparently no one could hear the music but me. Go figure. Yet, I was never behaviorally challenged. On the contraire, I was by all accounts quite independent and responsible. I delighted in taking care of my younger brother and being the surrogate housemother during my mom's illness. I did the majority of chores, performed well in school, and always carried the bulk of responsibility for ensuring things flowed well. I was always the crisis manager, the fixer, the she'll handle it person. Even by the age of twelve I was earning a pretty hefty sum of cash by babysitting neighborhood kids after school, and by sixteen I was working twenty hours per week in a local retail store. In high school, my principle hired me as a receptionist/assistant in the main office since I had earned enough credits by my junior year to have a very minimal number of classes. I was an honor role student and involved in every activity except sports (after all, I'm a girl to the third power). So what, if anything, was prodigal was a mystery to me.

Spending all my time in church didn't bother me much until I reached mid-teens. Before then, I didn't have much else to do. Besides, despite all the negatives, I still felt more significant in church than anywhere else. By my junior year of high school, though, I was kind of over the always-at-church thing. I wanted to discover a different world and find my place outside of what had always been our walls. I began feeling like there had to be something more to my person than just being the pastor's daughter, especially when according to others, I wasn't very good at that. So I started the process of trying to find out who and what else I was. This meant that I missed a few church events-prodigal. It meant that I developed more and more interests outside of church-prodigal. It meant that I didn't want to play the piano in prayer meeting or fill in for the bass player (*Yes*, it's true that I play the bass guitar), or direct the teen choir, or take on any more ministry responsibilities. This was deemed absolutely prodigal. I had nothing against church, honest. I was still a Christian. I still, for the most part, behaved in a Christian-like manner. But enough was enough. I was spent. I grew further and further away from the precedent that had been set by my older sister, and further from the expectation of who I *should* be. By seventeen, I was seemingly put on the equivalent of homeland security's orange alert status, because the church members had me under constant surveillance. They seemed to be everywhere I was, observing, reporting, tattling.

> Pastor, we spotted her at a nightclub
> Pastor, we saw her with so-n-so's son in the inner city, you know he's no good.
> Pastor, we saw her driving your car after hours; it didn't look like she had gas.
> Pastor, we're gonna pray for you cause' this one is gonna give you the blues. She's nothing like your other daughter.

Now, I can neither confirm nor deny the reports, especially since they're probably reasonably accurate. But none life-threatening, none worthy of front-page news, and none worth the lectures from my father! The final straw was when (still trying to find my place) I joined a high school sorority. That was apparently too much for any church member or Christian to handle. After all, church-mill rumor had it that these girls were known for being wild, promiscuous, cigarette smokers. This was all news to me! I knew nothing of these character discrepancies. I joined the group with the simple ulterior motives of wearing the cute little jacket & sweats with writing across the buttocks, dating one of the affiliate frat brothers, and getting in school events free. That was the extent of my membership. To this day, I've never inhaled or exhaled anything other than asthma meds, never smoked, never been drunk, can't dance, and don't like clubs. I only attended house parties because we sponsored them and because that's where my date was (also because I was a rapper in my day and had mad skills on the mic! But I digress). As far as the promiscuity, I graduated high school as a virgin. I had been to a total of three nightclubs in my life, twice under duress. Still, I was the perceived as the prodigal.

Funny thing was, I loved church. It was a big part of me, and I was a big part of it. But for many years, I felt disconnected. My gifts and talents didn't always seem to fit within the parameters of our ministry, so I strived to find venues where they did fit. Not instead of church, but in addition to. In my mind, what it boiled down to was that I simply wasn't good enough for ministry. At least not in my father's church. I was nothing like my sister; I didn't behave as she did. I didn't fit in like she did. I didn't have friends like she did. I didn't have her level confidence. I didn't possess her gifts (or so I thought at the time). I didn't have the same passion for ministry, and most significantly I didn't have the same desire to be at the center of everything. After all, the spotlight wasn't nearly as gracious to me as it was to her. So, I resisted the limelight. I didn't feel myself to belong there, and for me it simply was not fun.

It was thought, then, that one or both of my brothers would eventually take the helms of preaching, and my sister was already well on her way to ministry leadership. But I didn't feel such a calling on my life. If I couldn't even find my comfort zone in the church, how would I ever survive life in ministry? In my mind, these differences, these shortcomings, negated any chance that I would ever gain favor in the sight of my father, the pastor. In my mind, the whole church knew it. And in my mind, if my own father didn't favor me, why should they? If he made a distinction between me and the other children, why wouldn't they? If he insinuated, either intentionally or unintentionally, that there was a deficiency on my part, and that I didn't quite meet the standard, then why would the congregation draw any other conclusion. It's amazing what simple logic children use: *If my sister is in the center of ministry, she's good. If I'm not in the center of ministry, I'm bad. In my father's eyes, good wins over bad, and I'm just out of luck*! That was my thought process, but it got even deeper.

I clearly recall being disheartened when I first heard the bible stories of Cain and Abel, and of Jacob and Essau. I felt that I was Cain in a sense, because my gifts were unacceptable at the altar. I felt compassion for Cain that he gave the best he had, and that it wasn't his fault that his brother happened to possess the specific gift that God wanted. Now I certainly didn't condone the notion of him killing his brother, but I sympathized with his plight. After all, he wasn't a herder; he was a florist! He didn't have cattle. He had flowers and fruit. He gave what he thought was his best, but because it wasn't as good as what his brother gave, it was declined. At least that was my take on the story back then.

I was further disturbed by the fact that the Bible would record a scenario where one sibling could be loved, and the other hated, as such with Jacob and Essau. It was unthinkable to me that a father could hate their own child. But according to the Scriptures, he could…and he did. This story served as confirmation for me that such a thing could possibly be, and that it was happening to me.

Now I was pretty swift in the cognitive department, so I understood that the paramount principal in these stories were disobedience versus obedience, and not a highlight of sibling rivalry. I understood that Cain's consequence was due to his sin and disobedience to God, that it wasn't really about him having a less worthy offering. Yet these stories still seemed to reiterate the concept of one sibling being better than the other; one sibling's gifts being more acceptable that the other; and one having more favor than the other in the sight of their earthly father, and in the sight of God. And because for so many years I believed this to be my plight as well, I had a pretty miserable existence as a prodigal, an outcast, uncomfortable in my own skin, and without real worth.

Perception is paramount. It doesn't have to be accurate to be detrimental. In retrospect, I can't confirm how much of what I perceived about my world was accurate. What I can confirm is that my perception of that world shaped my feelings toward, and view of, the ministry. As a result, there was a part of me that resented life in the ministry. I resented the absence of my father as he seemed to spend the majority of his time at the church. I resented the undivided attention that he gave to the congregation. I resented the parts of my life that were missed, ignored, or de-prioritized because ministry came first. I resented the expectation to be perfect, all the time, and failing miserably. I resented the heartless remarks that church people would make about my family and me, and the insensitive things they would do. I resented people's evaluation and acceptance (or lack of acceptance) of me based on my being the pastor's daughter, rather than just Aundria. I resented being the pastor's daughter. I resented the shallow associations, the superficial friendships, and the paranoia that we only mattered because of the position we happened to hold. I resented the constant fear that life only existed in the walls of the church and that outside of those walls I would cease to exist. I resented the requirements. I resented the accountability. I resented the consequences. For years, I resented the call.

So there I was, now eighteen years old. Didn't fit in on the secular front, didn't fit in on the church front, and like most young adults, wasn't quite comfortable at home. I had no idea who I was, or why I existed. From the outside, I looked pretty good. I became skilled at downplaying negative feedback. I finally learned to make light of it, joke it off, suck it up, roll with the punches, and move on. Unfortunately, I never learned to let it go.

In the defense of others, there was no conspiracy in place to destroy me. I'm sure that neither my family members nor the church had any idea how I felt or how they impacted my feelings. I doubt there was any calculated plan on anyone's part to jeopardize my well-being or damage my self esteem. I didn't reach that place overnight, but I was there all the same. I was drowning in a state of low self-esteem, confusion, and what felt like total disconnection. I had reached a very detrimental point. Whether based on flawed perception or not, it was my reality, and I was pretty messed up.

Whatever occurs in their own lives, preachers kids are married to the ministry for as long as their parent is in the pulpit, and often longer. Some of us choose not to be a part of the ministry, but for better or worse, the ministry will *always* be a part of us. We will carry its wounds, its ways, its consequences, and even its rewards for the rest of our natural lives. And because we're human, we will often assess both the ministry and ourselves based on our perception of how the people within the ministry assessed us.

It was at a later crossroad in my life that I truly embarked upon the journey of discovering my purpose and God's plan. It took many years thereafter for me to find my identity. I continue to struggle with the world's view of who I am, versus God's view of me. But having survived the worst of times and come out on the other side, I am finally beginning to understand who, in Christ, I am. Moreover, he's fine-tuned my crisis management skills. He honored his promises: the water didn't drown me, the fire didn't consume me, and when the enemy came in like a flood… thank you, Lord, for raising up a standard!

The Looking Glass Theory

This brings me to the very noteworthy concept that I've been touching on all along. Years ago, a former member of our church who later became a minister and motivational speaker introduced me to a concept called the Looking Glass Theory. The theory suggests that we see ourselves through the eyes of others, yet *our* perception, and *their* perception, is often flawed. In short, the theory says,

> I'm not who *I* think I am
> I'm not who *You* think I am
> I am, who *I perceive* that *you think* that I am.

This theory piggybacks the idea of the self-fulfilling prophecy. Psychologists believe that we often become or take on the characteristics of whatever image of us is reinforced in our minds, either from childhood, or in another impressionable stage of our lives. If our parents tell us we're a failure, we may likely fail. If our parents tell us we're destined for success, we may likely succeed. We feed off of the positive or negative reinforcement of others, and that reinforcement can be direct, indirect, implied, or assumed. It's a sort-of mental programming that takes place, usually unintentionally, and we absorb and live it out, often subconsciously. You've probably heard some of this before, and it sounds logical, right? The biggest problem is not so much the negative information disseminated from person to person, but the fact that the messages we send and receive are often incorrect, flawed, or grossly misinterpreted. It's bad enough that our self-efficacy is largely rooted in how others perceive us. Even worse is that we're often wrong about those perceptions, which means that our self-efficacy is rooted in misinformation. And even if our perception of how others see us is correct, what's to say that they see us as we actually are? The result of these incorrect perceptions and flawed interpretations is a self-concept rooted in unreliable, unverifiable information. Imagine that our esteem could be rooted in lies. Imagine, from God's perspective, that it may be rooted in sin. Interestingly, this can work on the other end of the spectrum. We may take on the positive persona of how we think others perceive us. We may assume that others hold us in high esteem, and respond accordingly in our interaction with others. We see this all the time. The result of this overestimation of others' endearment may set us up in a false sense of security with our friendships, relationships, and public interactions. Whether the flawed perception is positive or negative, it gives us an obscured view of ourselves, and makes it all the more difficult to see through God's eyes.

This phenomenon played a crucial, often devastating role, in my life, and continues to do so in the lives of many young people whether under the spotlight or not. My childhood perceptions are rooted in the looking glass theory. How I perceived that my sister, my father, and others viewed me is how I began to view myself. It wasn't necessarily about what they really thought of me, but about my impression of what they thought about me. That's what contributes most to the shaping of our worlds. *We are who the most significant people in our lives think we are.* If not careful, we become beholden to these impressions.

The same results of perception are at work in the ministry. Being the first family of a sizeable church can be likened to being the first family in a political office, on a much smaller scale of course. All eyes are on you. You constantly find yourself in environments where everyone knows you (or knows of you), but you're at a disadvantage when it comes to knowledge of them. Each environment comes with an implied expectation of both who you are, and who you *should* be. Each individual within each environment has manufactured their own idea of how you should look, act, interact, behave, respond, etc. They evaluate your actions as well as your non-actions. They assign reasons and interpretations to everything that you say and do. They report their disappointment when you fail to engage per their standard, or when you inappropriately represent your role.

As the first family in a church, you're subjected to constant scrutiny. It's like living life under a magnifying glass. In actuality, you look the same as everyone else; but your flaws are magnified and made one hundred times more apparent by the many eyes that are watching. For example, right now I have a small scar on my hand that is barely visible to the naked eye. But if you zoom in and pay close attention, you can see it. If you fixate on it, it becomes unattractive, almost annoying. And if you place a magnifying glass to it, it instantly transforms into a major disfigurement that is not only embarrassing, but severe enough to want surgically removed.

We all have flaws that, to the unobserving naked eye, are minor and not worthy of conversation. Imagine if those flaws, whether physical or personal, are met with more observing eyes, and brought into the focus of your peers and the public. Imagine the ridicule. Imagine the scrutiny. Imagine the level of self-consciousness that would breed. Imagine the constant discomfort in your own skin. That's how it often is for us. That's life under the spotlight. Our imperfections are exaggerated and deemed so offensive that some of the lovely saints would suggest that they be surgically removed!

Another for instance. As mentioned earlier, years ago I was appointed as choir director by default (or so I thought) when the former director, my sister, shifted into the role of pianist. She still led the choir, but I was charged with the task of standing in front of them and directing the songs. It was initially the most frightening, uncomfortable experience of my life. She is an incredible music leader, and a gifted director. I was not. I lacked confidence, coordination, and the desire to do the job. The thought of standing in front of a group of people that were older than I, wiser than I (well, some of them anyway), and accustomed to her precision and expertise caused my heart to fail each time. To get through it, I would fixate on my sister as she played the piano and awaited her next instruction. In turn, I would communicate her instructions to the choir. It was quite obvious, and to them, it was hilarious. Thankfully, time bred a greater degree of comfort, and as she forced me to take on more responsibility, I settled more and more into the role. She was unconscionably cruel at times and harder on me than anyone else. But in retrospect, I appreciate her tremendously as she was responsible for cultivating a gift that I had no idea I had, and helping me grow thicker skin! I will always love her for that.

While I'd like to think that I exhibit a bit more skill and confidence in the music ministry today, I still struggle with the spotlight, and with perceptions. So, it occurred to me a few years ago to select a focal point whenever I'm in front of the choir directing, and fixate on it the same way I used to on my sister. The focal point I select is heaven. Seriously, the choir is facing the audience, but I'm facing the pulpit: and there is a certain spot on the ceiling above that I envision as heaven. I imagine Christ sitting on his throne in that very spot where my eyes land, and that he's observing my actions and assessing my worship. In times of true worship, I can visualize him standing up and welcoming my praise. Other times, he appears to remain seated, seemingly disappointed that my offering is apparently not for him, but rather for myself. Wow. He convicts my heart when my worship is not genuine, and reiterates that, spotlight or not, it's all about him-not me. He delights in those that will worship in spirit and in truth. He deserves nothing less; we should offer him nothing less.

Our youth pastor once profoundly stated that our music ministry should be for an audience of one. Jesus Christ. So my goal each time we sing is to focus on Christ alone as my audience, and to worship so genuinely, so completely, so wholehearted, with such humility, that my mind's eye can see him stand up, welcome me into his presence, and tell me that he's comfortable in mine.

Private Pain, Public Grief

Part of life as a ministry leader, a pastor in particular, is often having to pray your own way through, speak life into yourself, and wait to hear a word *directly* from the Lord. Thank God for all of the pastor's wives who hold the rope, pray their husbands through, and speak life into their spirit. My father had such a wife for forty-two years, and when she went home to be with the Lord, God blessed him with another. We can't possibly know as parishioner how vital such a companion is, and the extent to which it helps the man of the cloth survive.

It's been my experience that the most difficult aspect of life under the ministry spotlight is the grieving process. Pastors are the worst grievers, and their kids follow suit. Our process is incredibly flawed, so much so that it may appear as if we don't do it at all. For one thing, we're really expected not to grieve. That sounds ridiculous, but think about it. Imagine your pastor getting up in the pulpit one Sunday and breaking down, falling apart, unburdening himself on the congregation. The members do it all the time, but what if your pastor did? Service would abruptly end! The same goes for his family. What if I got up to direct the choir and lost it. What if our *tissue ministry* (seriously, we've got one of those) couldn't get the boxes there fast enough, and I cried inconsolably. Even if we were in some other venue with parishioners present, it would still be shocking, hard to respond to, and seem almost inappropriate. That's because our lives are spent encouraging others, helping them through their trials, and reminding them of the strength, comfort, and grace of God. You see, the pastor is the one that ensures us that weeping only endures for a night. He's the one that reminds us greater is He that is in you. He's the one that reassures us that when our mother and father forsake us, the Lord will take us up. So if he has all of the biblical reassurances, and the hand of God is ever on him, why on earth would he ever grieve? We forget that despite all the Scriptures, despite the intimate relationship with Christ, there's that pesky little thing again called being *human*. And as such, he, too, goes through storms. His family, too, experiences hurts. And we, too, question God's hand in the process. What? No faith? No assurance that the Lord will provide, that he'll bring you out, that he'll comfort you, that this is all for your good? Are you all the first family or what? Are you even Christians? Yes, yes, and yes. We're all of the above. But life still hurts.

What makes the pain even more excruciating is that when we hurt, we have to tolerate the pain publicly as well as privately. We wrestle with the need to preserve our testimony versus the desire to just be vulnerable and fall completely apart. There have been times when I didn't want to direct the choir; I wanted to collapse. There were times when my father didn't want to preach, he wanted to cry. We grieve on two fronts: the private home front, and very public church front. What's worse is that the church front is not just our own church, but all the affiliate and non-affiliate churches who fellowship with us, have a relationship with us, or simply know that we exist. This makes the grieving process awful. I can't think of more fitting word to describe it. Awful.

We still wonder to this day how my father can preach after a tragedy, or how he can minister to others at times when he, himself, needs to be ministered to. While we are continually amazed at his strength, we are baffled by the abnormal extent to which he is able to conceal his emotions. I was listening to my father speak in church one Sunday and the thought hit me like a ton of bricks: what happens when *he* needs to be ministered to? It rarely occurs to us that this would sometimes be. The pastor may need to be encouraged. He, himself, may be going through. He, himself, may need a word from the Lord. I thought of this because as he approached the podium that Sunday morning I could sense his heavy heart. It wasn't blatantly obvious, nothing he said or did made his pain apparent, but somehow I just knew. Maybe the Spirit of God told me, maybe I just know my father. But at that moment, I wanted to stop the worship service and have the choir begin minister directly to him. Yet, instead as always, he ministered to us. Our hearts were encouraged, our souls were fed, we went away rejoicing. I couldn't get to him after service that day because he departed immediately, and when I spoke with him later, he insisted that he was fine. I believe what he meant was, I'm better now.

My father would often share the memory of seeing his own father reading the bible at home in private one day, when no one else was thought be around. He observed his father reading, and praying, as tears hit the pages of his bible. My father learned from that experience that he could always go to God in times of trouble; that, like his own father, he could cry out to the Lord when no one else is around and rely upon God's Holy Word for answers. But I believe he also subconsciously extracted from this experience that *in private* was the only appropriate place to shed his tears. That quiet place, to him, is the only venue in which to share his most heartfelt emotions exclusively with the Lord. I believe that once he entered life in the ministry, he practiced a separation of worlds that kept grief and communion with God private so that he could effectively, publicly serve. His children learned this from him all too well. We learned to live publicly, and grieve privately. We learned to carry ourselves and our grief with dignity in the most difficult times, and to encourage others despite our own failing hearts. We learned to take our burdens to the Lord with the intention of leaving them there. Unfortunately, they don't always stay put! For better or worse, we spent our lives grieving alone. We mastered this technique of public pain, private grief. Crisis management to a fault.

Permission to Grieve

It seems insane that one would need permission to grieve. Grieving is not usually a choice, it's not a controlled phenomenon that you just decide to do or not do. Grief comes in many forms. We grieve our losses. We grieve our failures. We grieve our sins. We grieve our broken dreams. We grieve unexpectedly, and indefinitely. Though undesirable, it's normal. It's human. It's necessary. It's inevitable. We should never need another's permission to grieve…but in ministry, we often do. Perhaps unintentionally, others tend to set the bar for how we should go through our process. They deem what it should look like, how long it should last, how it should make *them* feel, and how we should come out of it. After all, our testimony is at stake, right? We're supposed to be Christians, leaders, men and women of God. We clearly should have the inside track, the Gospel advantage, the spiritual know-how, to grieve properly (in such a way that encourages others and creates the illusion that whatever happened really wasn't that bad at all). We're expected to grieve well. Amazingly, I get why this is so. I understand that when the first family is ill at ease, it makes others ill at ease. I get the notion that if *we* can't recover, then how can *they*. I totally understand the concept that if God won't heal *us*, who will he heal? Our testimony is at stake. Our convictions are at stake. All the world is watching to see how we'll recover, as an indication that we are truly who we say we are, and that God is who he says he is. Wow! That's a huge burden to carry... especially atop of a broken heart.

Please know that every ministerial family earnestly appreciates the support of their congregation during hard times. We not only appreciate it, we count on it. It's our lifeblood during those times. The congregation becomes our access to the throne when we find it difficult to pray; you become our consolation; you become our motivation for recovery so that we can get back to serving you, and serving God. Despite the difficulty of public sorrow, our home church has been a tremendous blessing time and time again as they stood in the gap during our darkest hours, and seemingly willed us through. Yet, it's that private time that we long for. That right not be okay, and for that, in and of itself, to be okay. We need the opportunity to determine how we feel, and why. The opportunity to vent. We long for approval to be human, and to be viewed as such. So that just in case we don't grieve quite right, we don't have the added burden of answering to the world for failing to weather a storm correctly, in addition to the burden of the storm itself.

Thank God, there are some in our extended Christian family who absolutely grasp this. Even when they don't know what to say, or what to do, they comprehend our plight. They don't judge. They don't question. They don't assess expectations. They simply pray. They encourage, they love, and they pray. For the faithful few who get it, know that you are a blessing. Thank God for you! May he show you favor, always.

That's life under the spotlight. So here are our little secrets for coping.

Coping Method 1: Thick Skin

One coping method that we develop is a very thick skin, which is either inherited or grown. My father has this attribute, perhaps developed in the military, or quite possibly through life experiences as a whole. Whatever the case, his thick skin was reinforced by a confidence that he's operating in the will of God. In the most difficult of times, he stood firm in his convictions as long as they were supported by the Word. I can recall so many times when, based on his convictions, he went against the grain; against popular opinion; against norms and trends; against what may have been politically correct. Whether the issue was as simple as appropriate attire or as controversial as fornication and homosexuality, he stood his ground, flat-footed, and preached the Word. While I'm sure he felt the pressure of opposing viewpoints and pushes for change, what I witnessed, what we all witnessed, was an unwavering stance for scriptural truth. As a result, he earned a sound reputation and high level of respect both within and outside of the church populous. I've always admired him for that.

Thick skin in this case does not mean indifference. It is not indicative of a lack of concern, nor does it suggest detachment from the situation. We can't detach from ministry. This is our life's work. It's what we're called, ordained, and impassioned to do. We're anything but detached, emotionally or otherwise. We see, we feel, we care, we're impacted more than the world will ever know. Thick skin is similar to a bulletproof vest: if you're shot in the chest while wearing one, you're going to feel it! And depending on the power of the weapon, it's going to hurt-likely even knock the wind out of you. You may even hit the ground pretty hard. But the vest, if it works properly, will save your life. It doesn't shield you from impact, rather it helps avoid permanent or terminal damage.

The reinforced layering of thick skin allows for enough distance so that we can maintain focus, and are not persuaded by the discontentment of others to give in to their demands. After all, there are so very many others, and so very many demands. Our church has more than fifty auxiliaries, each with their own mission. They sometimes tend to operate as little churches within the church. Each auxiliary has tens of hundreds of people. Each person has his own interest, his own viewpoint, his own relationship (or lack thereof) with the church and with Christ. Each auxiliary is made up of humans. Humans with their own mind-set, their own issues, their own personalities, their own motives. Hence, there's going to be discord. There are going to be conflicting viewpoints. There's going to be dissension in the ranks. Unfortunately, ministry leaders will surely be the targets of most, if not all, darts thrown. Absent of thick skin (that bullet proof vest), a leader is less likely to survive the impact. That's the reality. Ministry can eat you alive and discard your carcass, all in the name of the Most High. Thus, *loving at a distance* is not optional, it's mandatory. Over-sensitivity and/or wearing the heart on one's sleeve will severely undermine a leader's ability to lead with authority, and may ultimately render him ineffective. Relationships in ministry must also be routinely examined. Not only must the leader stay insulated as possible from the impact of self-interests and public opinion, his family must insulate themselves as well. So many times pastors and families are hit by *friendly fire* and assassinated from within. We're on the front lines and extremely vulnerable. Thus, it is imperative that we take on the whole armor of God and the covering of common sense!

If thick skin isn't a natural attribute, it needs to be prayerfully developed by every pastor, every leader, and every first family.

Coping Method 2: Role-play

Because my skin was not as thick as it needed to be, the coping gift I exercised most effectively over the years was role-play. The art of role-play requires that you learn to behave, react, and interact precisely the same in every environment. It's ironic because all through school I wanted to be an actress, but I had the most difficult time mustering up extreme emotions. I had so trained myself toward neutrality as a function of my life in the church, that I couldn't step out of the neutral zone to be something else.

Thus, role-play is deeper than Broadway. It's harder than following a scripted performance that changes based on the setting. It's quite the opposite. It's learning to exhibit the same persona, all the time, in every scenario, without being distracted by the reality of the situation. I mastered this. Regardless of whether the room is filled with friends or foes, my interaction is the same. I learned to govern my surroundings, and zone out the negative. I learned to transmit the illusion of confidence despite my often low self esteem, and to raise my self efficacy enough to insulate myself from any visible impact of criticism. Notice that I said visible impact. Because unlike having thick skin, role-play just exhibits wellness; most of the bullets go right to the heart! Unfortunately, role-play is just that- a role that one plays. It's mostly an illusion. It's not real. It doesn't last. It doesn't block the pain, it just sets wounds and offenses on the back-burner to be dealt with at a more appropriate, more private time.

The world's position is, *I'm real. I gotta be me.* But if the *me* that you are is not always conducive to the office you hold, then you must find an alternative *you* while the Lord perfects your essence. Otherwise, you're going to have to find a new office! In my case, changing offices (or ministry environments) was not an option. This tour of duty was appointed by the commander in chief, himself. So, role-play became an important skill to exercise while the Lord molded me into the person that he created me to be, which will ultimately be more appropriate for his ministry. I can *be the real me* when he matures me to the place where the real me is acceptable for his ministry. Until then, my sinful, human nature will always leave me vulnerable and hinder my testimony. Hence, I suspect that role-play may be my coping mechanism in ministry, and in life, for quite some time.

Obviously, the severe downside of role-play is its habit-forming nature. It's difficult to transform from role-play to intrinsic mode, and even more difficult to function in complete reality. This breeds tremendous challenges in interpersonal relationships, personal growth, and life outside of ministry. In fact, all life becomes identical to ministry life.

Role-play makes parenting a child who is also born into the ministry atmosphere a little tricky. Children mimic what they see, although they are amazingly gifted at distinguishing behaviors. Without me intentionally teaching her, my daughter learned very early on how to behave in various environments. Yet, despite my role-play mastery, she was cunningly able to decipher between church mom and home mom. Yikes! As a young teen, she began to resent the demands that ministry placed on her own life. People expected her to be like me, to react like me, to be polite like me, to be appropriate like me, to be the pastor's daughter like me. The thing is, she wasn't a role-play connoisseur. She was more authentic, more true to herself. More like a normal child and teenager than the rest of us were ever allowed to be. The problem was that our church world wasn't accustomed to her candor and she suffered dearly for it. Wow. The most painful reality was not the impact that ministry had on *my* life, but the negative impact that it had on *my child*. Furthermore, how I perpetuated that negative impact by always being ministry oriented. My home was not the proper venue for role-play. My job as a mother was to reinforce Christian behavior, not church behavior. My parental responsibility was to validate the person that my daughter is, rather than the person that our environment dictated that she should be. I dedicate an entire chapter of this book to the distinction between the two orientations: ministry orientation versus Christ orientation. Praise God for enlightening me. I trust that it will enlighten you as well.

Marriage was the ultimate challenge in converting from a lifetime of role-play to a life of reality. When we arrived in our new home after the ceremony, he actually expected me to shed the outer wall and let him experience the essence of who I am. Imagine that. He wanted me to just put myself out there-just like that. He actually thought a wife should be fully transparent with her husband for the benefit of the marriage. Go figure. Whether his expectation was reasonable or not (and by the way, it was), remember: all environments and situations were processed the same. My interaction was the same. I recall being horrified to learn of his initial impression of me from a distance. He thought I was a total flake! Imagine that, intelligent me, a flake. Ironically, I was even more horrified to see the person that I actually am, separate and apart from the *role*. That's what marriage does. It serves as a constant mirror that reflects your present image, and reveals your true self. It was so sobering that at first, I didn't even recognize her. I had no idea who this person that my husband revealed to me was, and once I was introduced to her, I couldn't imagine why on earth she was his pick! Was he sane? Was she that cute? What was he thinking? We spent the first year of marriage with him unwittingly teaching me all about Aundria and me objecting to the new information. Year two was spent reviewing the information, and again objecting. Year three, well, you get the picture. My goal, though, no later than year ten, is acceptance; embracing of the positive, and prayerfully transforming the other stuff. Bare with me, hubby, change is coming.

You see, role-play doesn't require you to fix stuff right away. You have the option to simply conceal the undesirable stuff until it can be rectified at some later date...in the future...when you have a free minute...and you feel like it. While it has the potential to be very instrumental in ministry, and has served me quite well over the years, role-play proved to be non-conducive to both marriage and family. I continue to struggle as I remain under the influence of both worlds. And since the ministry world is so much more familiar, and now so much more normal, my tendency is to gravitate toward it as my comfort zone rather than nurture a more transparent life at home.

With that said, time is running out. My first family tour of duty is set to end any day now, and the world I've always known will soon cease to exist for me. I'm prayerfully accepting this reality, and trusting that the Lord will acclimate me to what is now my primary ministry, my marriage, my family, my home.

I can see the hand of God guiding me toward a more transparent, authentic existence. I love him for that.

Coping Method 3: Willful Transparency

The most blessed and arguably effective coping mechanism that we can implement is willful transparency. Willful transparency is the ultimate place of freedom. It's a level of contentment that results only from maturity in Christ. It's a place where your nature is in tune enough with the nature of Christ; where you rest so confidently in him that you can become open and vulnerable to the world without regard for repercussion. Willful transparency lays all of you on the altar and lets the chips fall where they may. It reveals the good, bad, and ugly-not out of pride, but with a spirit of humility that is fully aware of one's shortcomings, but is wholeheartedly striving for holiness. This is a place of repentance; a place of brokenness; a place of restoration; a place of relief; a place of sheer peace. It's where God has molded, shaped, tested, and worked into submission your very soul, the essence of your being. He has refined your character, and established your security. Willful transparency comes about when the Lord has performed a such a work within the depths of your being that you become a blessing and benefit to others without regard for what they might give in return. In allowing them to see you for all that you are, and all that you've been, and all that you desire to be, you become a testimony of God's unconditional love and relentless grace. Here is where his plan truly unfolds in your life, and you finally surrender all.

After thirty-nine years of both voluntary and involuntary role-play, my heart's desire is for willful transparency. I realize now, that while role-play may have served a reasonably functional purpose through most of my years in ministry, while it protected me from certain emotional devastation, it did very little to develop my testimony. What I considered a necessary defense mechanism has ultimately resulted in an overwhelming sense of confusion, discouragement, fatigue, and loneliness. Role-play has drained me to the very core of my being. In many ways it has left me insecure and unstable, causing me to continuously revisit the questions of who I am in the world, and of who I am in Christ.

Only recently has the Lord begun to reveal the devastation that my commitment to this nonsense has caused. Only recently has he begun to reveal the person that he intentionally created. He's revealing my unique potential, my value, and my worth. He's causing me not only to be comfortable in my own skin, but importantly, to rest in my identity as his child. After all of these years, I'm finally beginning to fully realize and appreciate the unfailing love of Christ. Even as I write the words on these pages, I am settling into my designated place in the kingdom, by the grace of God. It's still amazing to me that I have any right at all to such a destiny.

Earlier I mentioned the difficult part of marriage being the shedding of former illusions and uncovering of undesirable characteristics and baggage from the lifetime before. What I didn't emphasize was the extent to which marriage can also uncover-even highlight-your gifts, shed light on your strengths, and offer a reflection of your spiritual destiny. For me it did just that. It gave me courage to confront my shortcomings, and celebrate the areas in which I excelled. It's so easy for the enemy to use our flaws against us to hinder our marriage, our ministry, and our mission. Thank God that instead, he allowed my own marriage to help gently guide me toward the willful transparency that not only pleases Christ, but causes me to understand and implement his plans for my life.

Only in reaching a place of willful transparency was I able to transfer a lifetime testimony from the pages of my heart, to the pages of this book. This book, then, represents my first quantum leap from role-play toward a transparent Christian life. To God be the glory, great things he has done!

A Word to the Wise

For those of you in or outside of ministry who have become academy award winners in your public life, only to find yourself unable to comfortably acclimate yourself to your private world, my prayer for you this day is that you will, first and foremost, come to a saving knowledge of Jesus Christ. I pray that you will realize the most pertinent position you hold, more important than any public or church office, is your birthright as a child of the King. My final prayer is that you redefine yourself and your self-worth based solely upon your blood connection. You possess infinite value simply as a function of being his child. The Bible tells us that we are a chosen generation, a royal priesthood, a peculiar people (1 Peter 2:9, KJV). Webster's Dictionary thesaurus emphasizes the word peculiar with the synonyms: *distinctive, uncommon, exceptional, extraordinary, fantastic, incredible, particular, special.* This is what God thinks of us! This is his perception. This is what he sees under the magnifying glass. This is what he views in *his* spotlight. This is his summation, interpretation, and conclusion of who we are. Why would we dare settle for, strive for, or pretend to be anything else? How could we not be comfortable in our skin? How can we hang our heads low in shame over perceptions of others, or be even remotely impressed by the opinions of man? The highest, most significant voice in the universe has prescribed our person and ordained our eternal good standing. What more do we need for validation?

As we wind down our days under the tremendous spotlight of ministry and prepare to leave our church home, I must constantly remind myself that no matter how many eyes may be watching, the only relevant view is that of my Lord. If he is pleased, then all is well. My eager desire is to continually see myself through God's eyes; to repair the attributes of my character that he deems detrimental; and to celebrate the attributes that will glorify him. I want to finally accept the notion that, I am fearfully and wonderfully made (Psalms 139:14a, KJV). Despite what the world's spotlight may reveal, God views me through the blood of the Jesus Christ, and through the lens of the cross. Hallelujah.

So then, it's time to get out from under the spotlight and establish our self-efficacy on the foundation of Christ. Regardless of how frequently and how relentlessly others make issue of our imperfections, be reminded that, *"There is therefore now no condemnation to them that are in Christ Jesus"* (Romans 8:1, KJV). Praise God, from this point on, we are free.

A Necessary Condition

Years ago, while I was in the midst of one of the most trying experiences of my life, my mother began to explain to me a concept that she called my necessary condition. A necessary condition is a circumstance, a situation, a life experience that is either part of God's divine will, or his permissive will, and is designed for the purpose of effecting spiritual and practical growth. Sometimes necessary conditions come about as a result of our disobedience, and fall in the realm of God's permissive will. This was my case. Other times, necessary conditions are specifically orchestrated by God as part of his divine will and plan for our lives. They may be a means of preparing us for what's to come; enlightening us on what has already taken place; perfecting us for kingdom work; enhancing our testimony so that we can minister to others; or simply demonstrating God's power and glory through our lives. Quite possibly, it may not be about us at all. The Lord, in his sovereignty, will sometimes take us through a situation or storm for the spiritual benefit of someone else. Imagine that!

I must admit that I can be a pretty hard case in the lesson-learning arena. If you're like me, you have to hit the brick wall not once, but until your entire front fender is bashed in and falls off before you swallow your pride and admit that perhaps there's a better way. Without the necessary conditions in life, most of us would never get from the place we are to the place the Lord desires us to be. Thus, necessary conditions are not optional; not desirable; and usually not avoidable. They're necessary. If we submit to God's plan, though, the outcome is life-changing, rewarding, and accelerating. We're launched to the next spiritual plateau, and to the next growth phase of our lives. Now we're useful to the kingdom.

Remember the scripture that I mentioned earlier that my mom would always repeat to me: all things are lawful, yet not all things are expedient; all things are permissible, yet I will not be brought under the power of any (1 Corinthians 6:12 and 10:23)? I was too young and stubborn to grasp it the first one hundred or so times I heard it, but here's what it meant in a nutshell:

> I'm an American. And as such, I have certain inalienable rights. As an adult American, I can pretty much do whatever I want to do. However, everything that I may want to do is not the best thing for me. Much of what I may want to do may prove detrimental to me. And some of what I may want to do may result in my demise. Therefore, I should carefully, and prayerfully, choose my actions, and not be unduly influenced to do those things that are not in my best interest; that are not profitable for the kingdom; and that will not glorify Christ.

God bless her for her wisdom. She knew I'd figure it out some day.

My Necessary Condition

An independent choice on my part to have premarital sex at the age of nineteen resulted in an unexpected pregnancy. I specified that the choice was independent because anyone who knows me knows that all of my choices are independent. I've rarely, if ever, been the victim of peer pressure, group think, or persuasion power. As much as I would love to say that the devil made me do it, I'd probably be giving him way more credit than he deserves in this particular case!

Anyhow, if you've ever watched the *Maury Show* on television which comes on five days per week and dedicates at least four of those to ridiculously dramatic DNA testing to establish paternity for buffoonish young guests (it's okay if you watch it, we can be embarrassed together) you can relate to the conversation I had with myself when I learned I was pregnant:

> I can't possibly be pregnant. I only had sex one time! My friend Kalisha has been having sex since we were in junior high school and she never got pregnant. Besides, I didn't think I could have kids because my great-grandmother on my mother's side was sterile when she was my age, and didn't have kids 'til much later in life. Not only that, but we thought about using a condom and only decided not to at the last minute. In any case, my dad is a pastor, so God will probably make all of this go away. Actually, I don't think the baby is even mine 'cause the ultrasound looks nothing like me! (Okay, I just threw that one in because I thought it was funny).

Yep, that's the crisis logic of a teenager. While I never questioned paternity, I most certainly questioned how on earth I could be pregnant. At that age we're like a deer in headlights when we get caught doing wrong; our mind sort of freezes up and we turn stupid. But ridiculous logic is how you work through things when you're young and in trouble. Either you explain the situation away, or stick your head in the sand and wait for it to go away on its own. My head stayed in the sand for seven of the nine months.

Humor of the situation aside, the events following my positive home pregnancy test were both devastating and life changing. Picture it: the pastor's daughter is pregnant... in a prominent church... a spotless reputation in church and community (his of course, not mine)... now this. It wasn't until my second trimester that I exited denial and finally accepted my situation. By month six, rumors were circulating that I could possibly be pregnant. Thankfully, a nineteen-year-old can conceal a pregnancy quite well. Despite my discretion, the lovely members of the congregation would unexpectedly appear at my job (the only public place I would go) to get a glimpse in order to confirm my condition. I knew that it was only a matter of time before word reached my parents, so in month seven I told my mother (Yes, month seven! And only after she asked!). I can't recall exactly how the conversation went, except that I remember her being amazingly calm, almost catatonic. She may have asked one or two follow up questions, including what my intentions were. She gently insinuated that abortion was not an option in the event that I'd given that any thought. I had. She instructed me to see a doctor because she knew me well enough to know that I wouldn't have otherwise done so and risked leaving a paper trail. Then she walked away. That was it. I could see her pain, her disappointment. I actually felt her heart breaking as if she had taken it out and placed it in my hands. For the first time in seven months, I cried, hysterically. Perhaps more for her than me, because I knew that this was the ultimate blow. I'd finally done what I worked so hard all my life to never do, disappoint my mother, and hurt my father's reputation. How did I manage to accomplish both so efficiently, and all at once?!

With a single choice, in a single moment, I had broken a family covenant. I felt like I had destroyed all that we were and ruined all that we'd ever be. I felt like the Lord would never be able to use any of us again. We were tainted. We were damaged... all because of me. I knew that I was an embarrassment to my father, and to the family. I couldn't fathom how he'd ever return to his office, much less the pulpit. Would they mock him? What would they say? What would *he* say? What could he tell a congregation that had caught his prodigal daughter red handed in a public sin? Everything they predicted about me was suddenly true. I was the weak link... the problem child... the worldly one... the screw up. How would my mom stand at the doors of the church after Sunday sermons and greet people with a broken heart? How could we possibly recover from this? How could we possibly go on? Why would we want to go on? I didn't want to go on. I wanted life to stop. I wanted to cease existing. I was ready to go to heaven, I feared that instead I'd go now go to hell. In any case, I didn't want to be here anymore. Not one day more. *But God.*

The Sunday immediately following this revelation, my mother gracefully went to podium about midway through the worship service and gracefully addressed the congregation. I had started working on Sundays several weeks prior to keep from having to attend church, so I wasn't present that day to hear her words, but countless people reported that her profound message to the congregation was as follows:

> As many of you are aware, my youngest daughter, Aundria, is pregnant.
> She is nineteen years old, and she still lives in our home.
> When we recently learned of the pregnancy, Pastor and I had three choices: We could put her out and let her fin for herself, we could orchestrate a shotgun wedding to try to publicly make things right, or we could simply love her, unconditionally, and rely on the Lord to sustain us.
> We chose the latter. We're choosing to show her unconditional love.
> We're choosing to extend that same love to her child.
> While we will not insulate Aundria from the consequences of her choices,
> We have forgiven her.
> We will embrace her, minister to her, and support her as she goes through this storm.
> We're asking that our church family do the same.
> Aundria is now on leave of absence from the church for an appropriate time.
> When the time is right, she will, Lord willing, come before you all for reconciliation and reinstatement in the body of Christ.

> Prayerfully, the church family will then restore her to ministry, and to the fold.
> May God bless each of you.

I will eternally love her for that. Thereafter, my father got up to preach. He stood flat-footed and preached the Word. After service that day, my mother stood at the door as always and greeted the congregation. They continued on in ministry: brokenhearted, hurting, embarrassed, discouraged, confused, and grieving their pain and mine. They were understandably fearful for what my life would become. They feared for my unborn child. The pain must have been overwhelming, yet they continued in ministry. They honored their call. On Monday, I went to my parents to formally ask their forgiveness and to thank them for their love and support. The hurt didn't stop for any of us then, or for a long time to come. But healing began. The Lord is good, and his mercy endureth forever.

It was several months later that my mother explained to me that this experience was my *necessary condition*. She put a godly perspective on a human situation, and ministered to me in a way that I can't even begin to articulate. It positively altered my perspective, and possibly saved my life. You see, we tend to think that when we mess up, we step beyond the bounds where God's love can reach and bless us. So far out of his will that he can't, or won't, heal and restore. The truth is, he already had a heads up on our situation, after all, he created us! He knows our comings and goings. He knows our makeup, our composition, and our essence. He knows our thoughts, words, and deeds even before we think, say, or do them. And because he knows and loves us unconditionally, his grace makes provision for any situation to result in our good and his glory. Please get this: *God's love is not contingent upon our obedience*. He loves us in spite of, not because of. This information is by no means an excuse to sin or vindication for our wrong choices. Rather, it is a celebration of the relentless grace of God!

I believe it was gospel artist Donald Lawrence who said, God will hold it together until we get it together. Absolutely true. Once God establishes a calling on our lives, he will use our self-inflicted trials as well as those trials divinely orchestrated by him to draw us closer to the place where he desires us to be. So, once you surrender your will to his, he can create an awesome result out of your biggest faux pas. Choices are absolutely yours, but ultimately, God is in control. He's got this. He's got you. He will come through every single time that you trust him. He will be true to his character, true to his Word, true to his Son's sacrifice on Calvary, and true to his promises to his children. I learned in my *necessary condition* that I am *not* the exception to God's faithfulness. I'm included in eternity. He intended his promises for me as well.

In the midst of this uncomfortable experience, my relationship with my mother was fermented. Mom was my sanctuary. She covered me. She worked relentlessly to reaffirm my worth, and get me to celebrate my person. She protected me from the attacks of others. She sheltered me from the rain, even at home. Through prayer, through encouragement, through nurturing, and through her godly example, she brought me back to spiritual consciousness. She fought the battles that I couldn't fight, and she helped me pick mine more carefully. She put out fires before they consumed me; she served as a floatation device when I tired of treading the troubled waters; she kept me grounded during the most unstable of times; she helped me overcome what seemed like insurmountable obstacles. My mother made a treacherous journey so much smoother. Time and time again-she saved my life. I shall honor hers forever.

Perhaps the most critical piece of wisdom she imparted during this time was the distinction between the Lord's divine and permissive will. She explained that although my choice was indicative of sin and disobedience, my child was not a mistake. God's divine will may not have included this path for my life, but his permissive will would allow for triumph. Considering all of the potential consequences that could have resulted from this unplanned, out of wedlock pregnancy, I marvel at what a blessing my child turned out to be. After all, she was my launching pad to maturity, and to a closer relationship with Christ.

Twenty years later, I still marvel at the outcome. Erica positively changed my life. She helped ground me. She established my priorities. She motivated me to succeed. She kept me out of sin time and time again. She enhanced my ministry. She increased my sense of responsibility. She gave me another reason to love, worship, and honor the Lord. In our family, Erica has served as the bridge that initially brought my sister and me together. And once my father healed from the emotional pain of my pregnancy, my daughter became our new common ground. More than he and I, the two of them forged an awesome relationship. He's her primary father figure. He was able to give her a much greater level of attention than he could his own children during their childhood since he was in a much more seasoned place in his ministry, with more control over his time. Erica served as a healing mechanism in so many ways. We thank God for her.

Let me pause here and say that as thankful as I am for the gracious outcome the Lord allowed, I don't wish my experience on anyone. Moreover, I don't encourage any woman, young or old, rich or poor, in love or not, to conceive children without the benefit of wedlock. Regardless of positive outcomes, we don't have the right to intentionally rob children of the benefit of both mother and father in the home, nor do we have a right to defy the Word of God, which gives us Christian ordinances regarding marriage and family. It is not our place to determine that our way is better than God's way. In making such a determination, we sacrifice the total well-being of our children and place them at risk for enemy attack. The Bible speaks of the sins of parents being visited upon their children. We see this over and over again today. This is the risk we take when we make sin choices involving our children, and their children. Not only are our offspring very likely to repeat our life choices, but they may forever carry our consequences and negative repercussions of our disobedience to God. Cover your children. Train them, protect them, and live such a life before them that they can draw on your wisdom and example throughout their lifetime. Prepare them for their own necessary conditions in life. Plant them firmly on the foundation of the Word of God.

Beware all Fixers!

Because necessary conditions can be agonizing times for ourselves and our loved ones, we may be tempted to fix it, to carry another's burden, to insulate them from the consequences of their sin choices or otherwise shield them from the experience. Here's the thing: We're not in control! We can put on the armor of God and fight. In fact, the Bible instructs us to do so. (Ephesians 6:11, KJV) But the battle is not ours. We're not fighting alone, and we can't win separate and apart of God.

Here again, I learn the hard way. Part of my makeup is being a fixer. I inherited this, too, from my father. Like him, I have a very low tolerance for inconvenience, and an even lower tolerance for observing those I love endure pain. When things are broken, I make sure they're immediately fixed. When there's a problem, I seek instant resolve. Dad takes it a step further in that he seems to absolutely delight in coming to the rescue. He takes pride in his ability to make things better, being the hero, rescuing the downtrodden, returning normalcy to a situation. That's who he is. Living with him for any period of time will undoubtedly transform any woman into the proverbial damsel in distress, because he gets a kick out of being the knight in shining armor. While growing up this was great! We were forbidden to do anything that had even the remotest hint of masculine work. We were girls for goodness sake. We weren't permitted to take out trash, shovel snow, or fix toilets. These were jobs for men folk. Either they did it or recruited someone else to do it. It was great, I tell you! I cherish those days.

We're an instant gratification, microwave society. So the likely thought process in a crisis will be: When will this be over? How long will this take? What can I do to resolve this matter more quickly and get back to my normal life? But growth processes are not fast food propositions-you can't have it your way. If you try to rush through the journey and avoid the inconvenience, the result will almost certainly be utter defeat, and having to start all over again. Remember when you would run through the halls in grade school to get to lunch, and the teacher would call you back to the classroom door all the way on the north end of the hall to make you start over, and walk? Then all your classmates would get to the lunchroom before you, enjoying the little strawberry shortcake bars and dry pizza that you loved so much way before you even made it in line? And then after waiting in line for ten minutes and finally reaching the counter, the mean lunch lady would inform you that they were all out of shortcake bars and nothing was left but spinach and rolls? Remember how frustrating that was? I vaguely recall it also. That's how it is when the Lord is trying to teach you something, and you rush through the process insisting that he hurry up and get to the point. You end up having to go back and start all over again. And by the time you get there, the strawberry shortcake bars (i.e. the blessings) are all gone!

Despite our programming for instant gratification, there are no cliff notes to the process of maturity. Short cutting the Christian maturity process may result in multiple storms, turning your would-be light shower into a tsunami! Interestingly, it's not just our own learning processes that we try to thwart; we get in the way of our loved ones' growth processes as well. My daughter, God love her, has led one of the most ridiculously sheltered lives that a child of a young, single parent with limited resources possibly could. I'm sure many of your children have too, because modern day parents are pitiful that way. You'd never know it by her constant murmuring, but she leads a charmed life. Forget silver spoon, hers is platinum! No inconvenience whatsoever. And like my father, I delight in resolving her problems, ensuring her comfort, and fixing whatever goes wrong in her life. I'll never know how much of her spiritual and practical growth I've stunted, or to what extent I got in the way of God's plan for her life. I do know, however, that many of her present struggles are a result of my well-intended sheltering. Now having to work through things on her own as a young adult in college, we're both engaging in an exercise of faith. I remain continually prayerful that the Lord will keep her. Regardless how uncomfortable her learning experiences, I must suppress my fix-it nature and get out of God's way.

Your Necessary Condition

Please know that whatever your situation, whether a poor choice with dyer consequences, the loss of a loved one, a financial crisis, a problem child, a health issue, or any other circumstance, God's grace is more than sufficient to see you through. He can heal your heart, and your land. The Bible says that, The end of a matter is better than its beginning, and patience is better than pride. (Exodus 7:8, RSV). I speak from personal experience when I say that tomorrow provides a completely new perspective and new resolve for the issues of today. If you can make it until the next moment, you can, and will, survive. We often seek permanent solutions to temporary problems, especially when gripped by fear. But we know from the Word that these light afflictions are only for a moment, that weeping endures only for a night, and that trouble does not last always. Get to the next moment. He'll meet you right there.

If you've messed up, and we've all messed up, I encourage you to forgive yourself, forgive others, and accept forgiveness from Christ. He shed his blood with your specific sin in mind, and covered you for your lifetime. As if that weren't enough, he designed a perfect plan for your life. Right now, he is orchestrating, approving, and governing the necessary conditions that will get you from the place you are today, to the magnificent place where he'll take you tomorrow. Rest in his Will. Take harbor under his wing. Your necessary condition is an essential part of your testimony, for an extraordinary work in his kingdom. Be encouraged. Be blessed. Be victorious!

Pain with a Purpose

Before I begin what will prove to be the most difficult portion of this book for me to write, allow me to share a piece of wisdom that the Lord has imparted to me in my journey: *Make sure that your pain has a purpose.* Don't permit your suffering to be in vain. Whether self-inflicted or a result of circumstances completely outside your realm of control, find the message. Not the *why*-that tends to be God's business. But prayerfully identify the lesson. And prayerfully try to get it the first time around. This won't cancel the pain, it may not even make it more bearable. What it will do, however, is strengthen your character, allow you to regain your footing, establish (or re-establish) your purpose, draw you closer to the Lord, and thrust you closer to your destiny. The alternative to attaching purpose to our pain is becoming consumed by it, and finding ourselves in a perpetual cycle of defeat.

Can you imagine if Christ's journey to the cross was without purpose, or if he didn't trust his heavenly father with the answers to the why's? Can you imagine if after it was all over he looked back and said to himself: *man, what was that all about? Hope I never have to go through that again!*' Not only would that have been a travesty for him, but for all those who are designated beneficiaries of Calvary-namely you and I. It's inconceivable for so great a sacrifice to have been in vain. Praise God, it wasn't! His pain was for a purpose. What made it so purposeful was that it was phase one of an even greater plan.

With that said, consider your pain. What if it's not just life happening to you? What if it's not just misfortune? What if it's more than a trial, more than an occurrence, more than a season? What if it is divinely appointed with an intended end? What if all of your pain, in your entire life, had a purpose? And what if in the end, that purpose is your spiritual prosperity? What if?

> Simon, Satan desires to have you, that he may sift you like wheat. But I have prayed for you, that when you come out, you will strengthen your brother.
> John 10:10 (KJV)

Whether you're in church leadership, a supportive ministry role, or whether you've not yet identified your spiritual call, please be confident that your trials are not designed to be fatal, nor are they in vain; they are temporary discomforts that can result in your permanent good. This story that I'llnow share with you is not for information's sake, but with the prayerful interest of encouraging you in Christ. I could not have shared this story 3 three years ago, I couldn't see the good. But today, I stand persuaded beyond the shadow of a doubt that my sifting, and the sifting of my family, was for the purpose of growing our personal testimonies, and to strengthen our brothers in Christ.

In September 2003, I woke up crying, and sat on the side of my bed thinking, *Either God is really upset with me, he's forgotten about me, or he has an awesome plan for my life because this storm just won't end!* Almost a year earlier my mother, my confidante, my heroine, my life support, my best friend, had gone home to be with the Lord (that's the only way I can process it. She's gone home, she's with the Lord. I can't call it anything else, I can't verbalize it any other way. No other terminology is acceptable. That's the only way I can manage to process her departure or stand the reality of the loss).

After surviving a terminally-diagnosed brain tumor thirty years earlier, giving birth to a son in the process, overcoming what was thought to be permanent, irreversible paralysis, and resuming a normal life, she seemed invincible. My family and I pampered her ridiculously in the years that followed, yet I don't think it ever occurred to any of us that she'd ever be sick again, at least not like that. Besides, she was the poster girl for the concept of 'blessed and highly favored!' In our minds, she would outlive us all just based on karma and biblical math. Even my father was convinced that she'd outlive him. He always reiterated very specific instructions with respect to the ministry and our family for when he's no longer here. I had already made up my mind to take care of my mother if, God forbid, that ever happened. She would come live with me, we'd find a new church home, I'd nurture her through her grieving process. We'd nurture each other, I'd take care of her. Plain and simple. For the rest of her life, I'd take care of her. I bought my house with this just-in-case plan in mind. All of this was settled in my thought process, but unfortunately, it wasn't written on High. The Lord had a different plan for her life and ours.

Sometime in 2001, my mother was briefly hospitalized for what was thought to be minor complications that may be mildly related to her tumor years earlier. After more tests, she was placed on fairly high doses of medications that she only semi-tolerated. She had several visits to the hospital over the next year. When her overall mobility became compromised, she spent time in a rehabilitation facility to try and regain basic motor skills, including use of her legs. Therapy and medications were apparently only minimally successful and she returned home from her final hospital stay in a wheelchair.

At that point, my father and I began to reconfigure our lives to accommodate her daily needs. We upgraded her chair, made adjustments to their home for her comfort and ease of navigation, and we assisted her throughout each day as needed. My father was her primary caregiver. He cut back substantially on his hours at the church and streamlined his other responsibilities to be home with her more. He met all of her needs. I was his respite, the secondary caregiver, and also restructured my schedule to spend most of my time at their house. My daughter took the baton regularly when my dad and I were absent and as another set of hands. We had a system. It worked. All was well. And life, for the most part, continued as normal.

By spring 2002, my mom's condition seemed to be deteriorating, and her upper limbs were weakening. Her appetite was decreasing, and independently completing tasks became more and more challenging for her. Without even realizing it, we reached the point where we were doing everything for her. We became her arms, her legs, her strength. We continued to modify the surroundings for her care, and continued to adjust our schedules to meet her needs. But for us, life was still normal. She was still normal, just not so mobile. She was still the center of our world.

Taking care of my mother was natural. It became routine. I actually enjoyed the excuse to spend exorbitant amounts of time with her. Perhaps it was so natural because I had been to this place before as a child, or perhaps because my relationship with her was just that close. For whatever reason, I preferred to be the one caring for her all the time. When she finally reached the point of needing a home health provider, I resented each one of them. I knew they had to be there when my father and I couldn't, but I hated it, and so did she. She would often refuse to eat until my father, my daughter, or I got there. I loved that. She would only want her personal hygiene needs taken care of by me. I loved that. She looked for one of us all the time, and only selectively responded to the care giving of others. You guessed it, I loved that. Eventually, the home health providers became nothing more than company for her until my father, my daughter, or I arrived. She stubbornly waited for us, and we tended to her as soon as we could. I observed my father's increasing fatigue as he served her round the clock, much more than we did. I watched his physical appearance change, and his spirit seemed very heavy. In retrospect I realize that he carried the weight of knowing the full details of her condition, and preparing for the inevitable. But I intentionally minimized it. Because to pay attention might require me to accept the fact that even if we were able to maintain this lifestyle forever, forever might not come. So, my daughter and I gave him as much relief as possible, and tried to make sure that he ate and rested sufficiently, and took his own medication. He didn't always. His heart became heavier, and his countenance eventually reflected a sort of helplessness-not in caring for her, but in her condition. I saw it, but I ignored what it meant. My siblings were less involved in the hands-on process, but they were often there. We were all there. We spent as much time as possible, right there.

In September 2002, my father sat us down and communicated the details of my mother's condition. Details that I didn't want to know and didn't accept: not then, not ever. I remember my siblings being upset that they weren't informed sooner. I recall the questions, the sighs, the tears. I recall actually singing songs in my mind as they were all talking. If I didn't pay attention, then it wasn't real. Then, the conversation was over. Something really strange happened in the days to follow... we all sort of returned to business as usual. Just like that. My siblings sort of disconnected from the reality of the situation. I, too, either went into denial or convinced myself that the same miracle that happened before would happen again. She'd be fine. Blessed and highly favored, remember? We'll all be fine. So, my father, Erica, and I continued the process of caring for her. We returned to our strange kind of normal. When she felt up to going to church, we took her to church. When she could go out, we took her shopping and to lunch. When she wanted to go for a walk through the neighborhood, or to the park, or to a local garage sale (she was the queen of thrifty!), we simply settled her in her wheelchair, packed up the water bottles, and off we went.

I recall when she began to struggle to sit upright or to move the fork from her plate to her mouth. I remember sitting very close to her in church so that when she would loose her balance, she could lean on me without anyone noticing. I remember feeding her, but insisting that she take every forth bite on her own to get her using her own hands. She struggled, but she did it. And I believed she was getting stronger. I remember my daughter and I putting her in the bathtub and massaging her legs in the warm water while bathing her. We'd have her circulate her own feet and lift her legs as much as possible without help to get stronger. I remember holding her up and making her take as many steps as she could from the bathroom to the bed without the wheelchair, so she could get stronger. I recall how tired she would be, and how frustrated she would be with me, but she'd do it. She'd do all of it. And to me, this meant that it was only a matter of time before she was completely healed.

In late September I enrolled the three of us, Erica, my mom and me, in an aquatic exercise class scheduled to begin October 15. We were scheduled to go twice a week from six thirty to seven thirty in the evening. This would help strengthen her legs and allow her to move about more independently. Now this was a tremendous sacrifice because, as you may know, women of color often struggle with the hair and swimming thing. We purchased our caps and our swimsuits and were ready to give it a go. The plan was that I'd leave work early on those days in time to pick Erica up from school so we could get my mom bathed, dressed, and ready to leave her house by five forty-five p.m. on aquatic days. That was the plan. It was a good plan. Our plan. Not God's.

My mother started experiencing a considerable amount of pain in her legs and hip-so much pain that it became necessary to administer pain medicine to her via injection to give her relief. By October 11 my mother was bedridden. Moving her became too painful for her. She'd completely stopped eating, and slept most of the time. I spent my time at the house laying next to her. I'd sing. I'd recite scriptures. I'd talk to her about everything that was happening in my world and everyone else's. I held her. I waited for her to get better, believing each moment that tomorrow would be a better day. By the evening of October 12, she was no longer responding to me verbally. Her breaths were heavy and stressed. Each time I touched her she shrieked; the pain had intensified so that she was sensitive to even the slightest contact. She was clearly uncomfortable and seemed only minimally aware. I laid next to her as close as I could without causing her pain. I sang every hymn I could remember (and believe me she taught us many). I recited every scripture that would come to mind. I even sang the lyrics of her favorite song, My Father Planned it All. That was the song she sang when she was at this place so many years ago, and the song that would somehow bring her out again now. I saw her condition, I was right there. But I kept believing that it was temporary. I recall hoping she'd feel well enough to attend our first swim class next Tuesday.

We never made it to aquatics class. When next Tuesday came, she was gone. God took my mother to Glory on Sunday morning, October 13, 2002. She went peacefully. She went in her bed. She went in my father's arms. She went on her favorite day of the week, the Lord's day. If you've ever lost someone close to you, you can relate to my mental state following news of her departure. My mental state at that moment was something like this:

Dad called my sister first. I hated him for that. My sister went to the house, and from there called me at home. I hated myself for having left the night before. I hated her for getting there before me. I hated myself for not seeing it, not realizing that mom was dying. I hated my mother for leaving me without notice. I hated God for taking her. He could have healed her. He could have fixed this. She did everything right. We did everything right. My father did everything right. He served God faithfully in the ministry. So did she. So did all of us. We weren't done. She wasn't done. Okay, maybe we screwed some stuff up, but give us a few more years and we'll do better. Okay, what about a few more months. I'll even settle for days. Don't do this. God, you have no right to do this. Forget sovereignty, this is our lives you're messing with. You have no right. We don't deserve this. It's not fair. It's not love. It's hatred. It's vindictiveness. It's mean. I'll never forgive you, God. You'll never be able to make this right. None of us will forgive You. Don't talk to me anymore, God. I'll no longer talk to you, or about you. I don't love you anymore. And you can't possibly love me. That's understandable. I can be unlovable. But why don't you love my father? He's one of the few good servants you have in these last days, and this is how you treat him? This is how you love? How is that love? How is that for his good? How is any of this good? Is it for your good? How? How can this possibly be good for you? Are You that selfish that you'd take her for your good? You promised not to give us more than we can bare. This is more than we can bare. That's it. I'm done. I'm done with you. I'm done with church. I'm done with life. I'm coming into your presence unannounced, or not, I don't know. I don't care. I'm done with faith. You know my father won't survive this, don't you? God, please don't take him too! Okay, that's my last request, my last prayer. Please don't take my father too!

By ten a.m. Sunday morning everyone started calling. That's when my family and I officially went into shock and began functioning on auto pilot. My younger brother was still at his apartment in New York and my older brother was at home in Columbus. It was just my sister, my father, and I. Her husband and family came later. They brought my daughter. I didn't have the emotional fortitude to tell her, so I'd left her home, asleep, and let my brother-in-law pick her up and bring her to my parent's home later on. He told her. She was inconsolable. She disappeared into a room at my parent's home for hours, maybe even for the rest of the day. I can't say for sure. I wasn't a very good mother that day.

My sister transformed into the perfect hostess, as if on cue, and stayed that way all week. It was a good thing because someone had to. I simply coped. My father restlessly grieved. People came. All day, every day, they came. The phone never stopped ringing, and the food never stopped coming. I've never seen so much food in my life. I would have killed for an appetite! We were the model first family. We were grieving right, we were grieving well. For now. We even consoled others that fell apart in our presence, over and over again, all week, we consoled them as they fell apart in our presence while we miraculously held it together.

The worst part had to be the arrangements. Dad gave me a budget and asked me to handle it. It was the hardest thing I'd ever done in my life. I cried as I prepared the program, I had an internal meltdown while writing my mother's obituary. I refused to consolidate her life in a traditional five-and-a-half-by-eight-bulletin, so we created an eight-and-a-half-by-eleven booklet. A total celebration of life, photos, inserts, memoirs, dedications, everything we could think of to appropriately honor her. Still, it didn't seem like enough. Even by the time I'd finished finalizing all of the details for the home-going service and burial, none of it seemed real. I was so far removed from the reality of this situation it was scary.

Seven days would pass until the home-going service took place. By the time my brothers made it later in the week, we were deliriously exhausted. We'd been entertaining around the clock for four days by then, and we just wanted everything to be over. My concern for my father was growing as I watched him sleep for only moments at a time, and pick over food without interest. I was also worried about my daughter, who seemed to be catatonic one moment and quite volatile the next. Her emotions were all over the place. I knew she needed me, but I had no clue how to meet her where she was. I had no clue where I was. I just wanted things to be normal. There was no time or space to process things right now.

There were so many people at the house during those seven days that we had a couple of guys from the church park and retrieve cars for our guests using a nearby community lot. We even had to notify the local police and fire department of the anticipated high level of traffic. It was insane. I don't recall how much I slept that week, but I never actually went to bed. When I dosed, she was in my dreams; she invaded every part of my subconscious. Waking up to reality was too hard. It was easier not to go to sleep. That went on for a quite a while. Perhaps weeks, maybe months. Just naps. No bed. No planned rest. I wasn't really planning to sticking around much longer anyway, so who needed sleep? My plan, at least my immediate plan, was to go and see my mother. I wanted to be with her again. Nowhere else. Just with her.

The services were at our church the following Saturday morning. I'm told that the night before, there were hundreds and hundreds of people at the viewing, which was also at our church. I'm told that when we exceeded the building capacity, ushers sent mourners to an adjoining building to view the service by satellite. I'm told that the funeral procession to the cemetery was more than a hundred cars; that must be true, because at least four different police districts, along with a horse-mounted police unit assisted in the escort.

Our choir sang. My sister played the piano. I directed. They ministered well, so I'm told, although I don't fully recall. More amazingly, my father delivered the eulogy-the most powerful eulogy he'd ever delivered. That I remember. He was phenomenal. I won't even begin to try to describe it because my description would not do it justice. But it was extraordinary. I'm told the service was a glorious occasion. A true home- going celebration . Everyone honored her well. Her legacy resounded throughout. They tell me it was extremely tasteful, appropriate, and fitting for the virtuous woman that she was. While I wasn't cognitive of all that took place that day, I can imagine that the reports were correct. Because that's how my family grieves. Dysfunctionally, and very well.

Then the next day came. And here's where pain must have a purpose.

Many of you can relate to this type of loss and to the wave of feelings and emotions associated herewith. It can be one of the most devastating experiences you'll ever undergo. Life is never again the same. In many cases, the initial loss is just the beginning. A series of domino effects often occurs thereafter that cause things to worsen for some time to come. Such was the case in our family. The home going of my mother set off a chain of events that tore the very fabric of our family unit, tested our faith to the fullest extent, and caused irreparable damage to our ministry. Here's where we confirmed, first hand, that a divided house will fall!

First, there was my father's grief. My mother was all that he knew. She was a part of his home life, his work life, his social life, his total existence. She represented his most significant past, and everything that existed in his present. She was his heartbeat, so evidently that my siblings and I believed that if one of their hearts stopped beating, the other's would as well. We almost called that one right! My mother took care of my father, and my father took care of my mother, to a fault. He took great pride in serving her. It was his pleasure to be her caretaker, even before she got sick. He accommodated every need she had, and pampered every aspect of her life. He provided for her. He ministered to her. He cared for her. And this validated him. Her love validated him. Her presence was his peace. Now she was gone. And he was completely lost. So, in the days and weeks to follow, he deteriorated rapidly. My daughter and I would go by daily to check on him (he didn't want us to sleep over); we couldn't make him eat, get dressed, take his medication, or care for himself in any way. He was in such a state of depression that he failed to notice a smoke detector beeping right above his head as he lay on the living room sofa one day. We heard it immediately when we entered the door and inquired as to how long it had been going off. He had no idea, nor did it seem to matter. I'm not sure my siblings quite grasped the severity of his condition. They saw him. They spoke with him. But I don't think they understood how far he had sunken into his state of despair, or how unlikely he was to come out of it. I wasn't as close to him at that time, but I must have seen his condition through my mother's eyes because it was quite apparent to me that he was in trouble. None of our attempts to console him were successful. And the more time went by, the worse off he became. Even after he returned to the pulpit months later (and I'm not quite sure how he returned to the pulpit months later) he was still in trouble. It bothered me that no one seemed to get it. They viewed him as superhuman, and minimized the extent of his pain. It was as if they thought he was too strong to hurt, or too spiritual to give up. Perhaps. But he came dangerously close, and I grieved his grief, constantly. More than for myself, I grieved for him. I hadn't really resumed fellowship with the Lord, but I couldn't help pleading with him to save my father's life. When others asked what my family needed, I told them we needed them to pray for my father. I told them he wasn't well, and that he needed Divine intervention to recover. I tried desperately to make my siblings get it, to get where my father was. And I believe that deep down they absolutely did, especially my older brother. But what could they do? What could any of us do? We were understandably so far gone ourselves that its reasonable to have missed some of the warning signs. All I knew was that another funeral was dangerously imminent, and I couldn't even begin to deal with that reality. But God.

The next sequence of events is unfortunate, almost unbelievable, but they happened. Prayers were answered, and my father finally took solace in the comfortableness of his relationship with a longtime friend of our family. However things developed, they developed. The result was that he slowly reentered his right mind, and seemed to regain motivation to get to the next day. This is all I wanted him to do, just make it to the next day. That's all we can do in times of grief: get to that next moment, exhale, and wait for strength to move forward again. It made no difference to me how my father got to each next moment, I was just thankful he did.

Celebration of his gradual recovery was apparently not nearly as important as the rumor that my father was spending time with someone. That information hit hard and circulated fast. The good old church gossip mill quickly got to work on adding to and subtracting from the truth, until even the characters involved were unrecognizable. Everyone was in an uproar. Everyone had there own objections, and their own reasons for objecting.

The most defining objection of all is what ultimately divided our house, because it came from within. My sister objected. And when she did, it affirmed, even justified, all other negative sentiments. So began dissension in the ranks and a domino effect of mass division. One year following my mother's home going, my sister announced her intent to resign as music director and leave our church to start a new ministry. She was not only our music director, but also the founding leader of our largest music body. For more than twenty-five years she was the face of our choir and an intricate part of our body. She was an essential member of the first family. She was my father's firstborn, his heart, arguably his favorite. She defined our family. She defined my role in ministry. She represented my comfort zone. Now this! I was devastated. Not angry, not even confused. Just devastated. Because it knocked the wind out of me, I wasn't prepared for such an evolution. I wasn't prepared for any of what happened next. Her announcement launched a most unfortunate series of painful separations. Some members left to follow her, some left in protest of my father's new relationship, and some left in disgust at the whole situation. They were simply disappointed in my family and our very public war. Many opted out of the line of fire. Even those who stayed became victims of our family mess.

The attacks on my father, our pastor, were vicious and continued for years to come. People attacked his character, his reputation, his pastorship and right thereto, his family, even his salvation. As if that weren't far enough, they questioned the genuineness of his affection for my mother. Forty-two years. Richer, poorer, sickness, and health. Loved, honored, cherished. Mutually kept every vow. Yet people had the audacity to tarnish the only thing he still had left in tact… the legacy of his relationship with my mother. That's when my gloves came off. No more role-play. No more thick skin. No more political correctness. No more accommodations. I went on the front lines in the battle to defend him, a battle that would last seemingly forever. At this point, it was no longer an issue of what he *should* have done, or what he *could* have done, or what his grief was expected to look like. It was a matter of his right to live, to love, and to continue serving God without compromising his holiness. So he did. He remarried two years after my mother's home going. And once again, all hockey sticks broke loose. Except this time, I was ready. I drew lines in the sand and dared people to cross. *Feel how you want to feel, believe what you want to believe. But I dare you to disrespect my father, my pastor, not in this house!* That was the prodigal daughter's position, and I must confess that for the first time, I didn't mind being just that.

In addition to attacking my father, though, people attacked my father's new wife. That was even more vicious. None of us were off limits: not myself, not my siblings, not my daughter, not even his wife's family. None of us were immune from the verbal weapons of mass destruction. That's exactly what they were! My father was villainized. My sister was villainized. My father's new wife was villainized. Our church was villainized. What do you do when you're caught in the middle, loving everyone involved, but grossly disappointed in their behavior? What do you do when the damn is breaking, and you can't block the flood? What do you do when the ceiling of your house is cracking, and the divide is imminent? What do you do when you know, beyond a shadow of a doubt, that for the first time in your family's history, the house will not stand. What do you do?

My resolve came from a simple scripture that kept resounding in my mind. Honor thy father and thy mother. There is no one in this world that my mother loved more than my father. No one she trusted more. No one that loved her more. What would she want me to do? What did God want me to do? Got it. That's what I did. Case closed.

As if the loss of my mother wasn't terrible enough, the loss of fellowship with my family was almost unbearable. Our whole lives have been lived in each other's company. Our family vacations, our Friday evenings, and Saturday afternoons, our Sundays were all spent together. Not only did we spend every holiday together without fail, we'd also spend the days just before and just after together. Thanksgiving always started on Tuesday. Christmas was at least a week. The first half of July was spent preparing for our family vacations; the second half was spent going on vacation. My mother, sister, daughter, and I had a standing appointment each Saturday in retail heaven with our favorite gentlemen: TJ (Maxx), JC (Penney), Brother Gabriel, Marshall, Dillard, and Mac(y). From time to time, we'd even visit Mr. Value, who lived in a wonderful city.

Though Fixers by nature, we couldn't fix this. We couldn't control it, we couldn't sugarcoat it, we couldn't put a spin on it, we couldn't make it better, we couldn't govern the outcome, and we couldn't turn back time. In preserving our defenses, we annihilated relationships and created a host of unintended consequences. We knew that no weapon formed against us would ultimately prosper- God tells us so in his Word. Yet, it became painfully obvious that we would have to remain in the fire for quite some time to come, and there were times when we were not at all convinced that we wouldn't be consumed.

Remember my brother, the peacemaker? He became crucial during the period following my mom's departure. He went to work right away on bridging the gap, and picking up the pieces of our broken unit. The politician, though distant, maintained clear perspective on the whole issue of my father's marriage and all of the verbal attacks on both sides of the family. He held the notion of 'innocent until proven guilty,' and remained as neutral as his strong convictions would allow him to. Most important, though, he remained open to healing and reconciliation.

We continue to grieve the damaged relationships within our family, but we are confident that what God ordains, he will maintain. We believe that there is still life amidst the rubble, and while it may take time, I hold fast to the hope of full reunion.

Despite what seems like a total loss suffered by my family, all of us are effectively rebuilding our individual lives, each of us still somewhat lost, and each of us somewhat resistant to change. The world we were born into was the only world we knew. We were the first family. We were the Hawkins family. We were extensions of one another, and we were defined by our role in the church. The notion of existing independently is overwhelming, and virtually incomprehensible. We had a hard time processing change. But we did. We're making sense of the situation, and finding effective resolves. We're finding a new kind of normal, so to speak.

Forgiveness Purpose

For me, forgiveness took years. There was forgiveness toward those that I *perceived* had subjected my father to undue pain and suffering. As crazy as it sounds, I even had to forgive my mother for dying.

In retrospect, this series of events forced the world to process my family in a new light. It bred the same discomfort with change for the church body as it did for us. They, too, were forced to consider a forty-five-year testament from a new standpoint, and witness the vulnerability of a once stable, seemingly invincible, legacy. Their world was also severely impacted, and their church home would be forever changed. Reactions were unfortunate, but human. The only way for the healing process to commence was for forgiveness to take place. For me, it didn't have to be mutual. It didn't even have to result in reconciliation, although I prayed for years that it would. I had to forgive to heal. Whether or not I was ever forgiven by others, I had to forgive in order to be forgiven by God. I had to forgive to fulfill his plan, and to identify the *purpose for the pain*.

So what was the purpose? Why the devastating process? What was the point? I believe that this was another necessary condition, not only for me and my family, but also for our church body. It was a life changing, accelerating experience designed to launch us to the next spiritual plateau. It was to take us into the next growth phase of our lives, and our ministry. For the church, this condition was necessary to weed out all that was not conducive for the future of the ministry, and to make room for new gifts to be unveiled. People are serving in vital positions in our church now that never would have assumed these roles under past regimes. Ministries are growing beyond past stagnation to a level that was not achievable in yesterday's culture. Our focus shifted from our leader, to our Lord. For what may have been the first time for many, we began to see our pastor as human. He's not the Christ. He merely presents the gospel of Christ to us. Humanizing him allowed us to become more transparent ourselves, and realize that but by the grace of God we would all give up, mess up, and meet defeat. There was almost an inexplicable calm within our church after this storm. It was as if the Lord had freed us, freshly anointed us, and given us a new reason to worship him. That's another thing. We're finally learning the true meaning of worship and how to fully engage therein. Imagine that ... we're Baptist, and we now worship!

The purpose of my family's pain was to break yokes that were no longer conducive to our individual relationships with Christ. What was once a comfortable place needed to become uncomfortable. The crutches of, and co-dependence on, our family unit had to be removed in order for us to rely completely and solely on Lord. We now had to go to God for ourselves, by ourselves. Mom couldn't do it for us. Dad couldn't do it for us. Our siblings couldn't do it for us. Instead of focusing our attention on good accord with one another, we each needed to be on one accord with Christ. Ministry and Christianity were no longer a group project. Wholehearted, individual participation was now required. And so began the process for individual relationships with Christ. Moreover, we needed to separate from our birth families, and begin nurturing and ministering in our present homes. You know, the whole leave-cleave thing? Before this, we didn't leave and cleave, we stayed and played. We never distanced ourselves far enough from our first family unit to effectively establish the new units that God gave us. And absent of this necessary condition, I suspect we never would have.

The purpose of my own pain was the most difficult to discern. It didn't take long for me to recognize what God was doing on a mass level, but it took years for me to make the application personal. I, too, married within two and a half years after losing my mother. I love my husband and thank God for our marriage. In retrospect though, it was a crisis-driven decision. I believe that part of my desire to wed may initially have been rooted in my wanting to get past the grief and on to a new beginning. I pacified my pain for years, filling my voids with ventures, projects, and new love. I was incomplete when I walked down the aisle, and my husband knew it. He was placed in the impossible position of not only having to rescue me, but forcing me to realize that I needed rescuing. Even more impossible was the fact that he operated from an extreme disadvantage. He was fairly new to our world and had a limited history to work from in understanding where I was, and how deep my wounds really were. It had to be the grace of God that navigated him through the jungle to meet me at such a devastating place, and that gave him the strength to carry me safely through. God bless him for persevering. God bless him for loving me enough to endure. My marriage was part of the purpose. It was also part of my reward.

Another part of the purpose was the revelation of my gifts. I couldn't initially understand why God would cause me to lose a relationship with my sister that took ninteen years to commence, and had only recently cemented. And why at a time like this when I needed her the most? Why wouldn't he cause her to be the one to stand in the gap for all of us? She was the oldest, she was closest to my father, and she was the strongest (or so we all thought). Why remove her from us too? There were times when I perfectly understood her position in all of this, I know her well enough to know exactly where she was coming from. But whether she was right or I, being right was simply not as important as our relationship. I wanted the relationship. In my mind, we needed each other to heal, what was happening was completely non-conducive to the healing process. I resented both her, and my father, for not seeing this. I resented them for placing me in the position of having to assume her roles and responsibilities at church.

Didn't God understand the sensitivity and discomfort involved with that? Didn't he know that she and I were nothing alike, and that I wasn't equipped to fill her shoes? So what was all this about?

Funny thing, it was apparently never important to God that I be like my sister, or that I possess her gifts. Apparently, he created me as a unique being with gifts of my own, and waited all my life until this point for me to pay attention to what he was trying to show me: my own worth; my own spiritual and practical gifts. I missed that message for thirty-five years. My mother delivered it, other ministry leaders delivered it, my husband even delivered it. But I missed the message over and over again. There was a place for me all along, but I couldn't see it. There was room for my vision, room for my contribution, room for God's hand to work in my life, room for my free and uninhibited worship. There was room for the prodigal daughter to be transformed into a vessel that God could, and would, use for his glory. Who could have imagined?

Who would have ever dreamed that God had a plan for me in all of this? Who knew that he would use the once deemed prodigal child to help restore and recover what was lost in the fire? Aundria, Lord? Are you sure? Is there a Plan B? Who would have ever dreamed that he would choose me to serve him at the forefront; that he would give me increase, that he would begin to heal my land. Even outside of my comfort zone, he would do it. Who would have ever imagined that all those years God had *me* in mind...me! He was designing a plan specifically for me! He would someday establish my leadership in the same body of Christ that had broken my heart time and time again; he would allow me to serve him, and the church, without apprehension. Who could fathom that favor of this kind really existed? He has so many other choices. So many more gifted choices. So many more worthy choices. Choices with fewer issues, less baggage, more maturity, less yuck! But he chose me. What a privilege, what an honor, he chose me.

But the purpose doesn't stop there. A lifetime of feelings of inadequacy with my father was erased the moment that we partnered in the intense care of my mom. For her sake, we needed one another. For her sake, we worked together. For her sake, we each depended on the other to make things better. We became co-fixers, partners for her wellness. My mother's prayers for our relationship were answered in the midst of her own crisis. My usefulness was finally established, and a whole new level of reverence for my father grew even in the worst of times. I finally began to count myself worthy of something. This was crucial, because until I began to see my own self worth, I was incapable of receiving or genuinely giving love. Please take a moment to ponder the multitude of blessings in that.

Yet another purpose of my pain was to learn to nurture, support and minister to my daughter. I relied upon my parents a great deal in the raising of Erica. My mom was a skilled disciplinarian that always made the punishment fit the crime. For example, I arrived at my parent's home to pick Erica up at work one day only to find her repeatedly walking up and down a flight of stairs. She was clearly exhausted and upset, but completely silent. My mom was sitting comfortably in a chair at the bottom of the staircase, casually leafing through a catalogue. When I asked what the deal was, my mom allowed Erica to speak long enough to explain: apparently she came in from school, ran upstairs and threw her backpack in the middle of the floor, then ran back down. My mom instructed her to go back upstairs and put to pick her bag up off the floor; Erica's response was to smack her lips, breathe hard, and stump her feet as hard as she could up the steps in protest. My mom's fix to this display of misconduct was to have her softly walk up and down the flight of stairs the number of times equivalent to each step she'd previously stomped on all twenty of them. It was great! Immediate resolve, never had that problem out of her again. Another time Erica thought it would be a good idea to write on the walls in my mom's sunroom. No reason, she was five years old, had new crayons, and just felt like it. My mother responded by admiring Erica's lovely artwork, then giving her a bucket of soap and water to wash all the walls in that room from the floor up, starting at the baseboards and as high upwards as she could reach. Ingenious! No more writing on the walls-ever. As a result, Erica was not only a very respectful child overall, but she revered and loved my mother dearly. With my dad, things were much simpler. He'd just look at her sternly and misbehavior would stop before it started. Easy enough. Because they were secondary caregivers for Erica and had so much of her rearing under control, I didn't have to contribute quite as much in the early years as I did later one when my mom was no longer here, and my dad was readjusting to life. I was suddenly forced me to become a full service mother. I had to become the nurturer, the full time caregiver, the sole support system, and the spiritual guide. That was the hardest. I now had the responsibility to train up my child in the way she should go. I had to become what I should have been all along...an effective Christian mother. That was a very significant purpose of my pain.

Looking back, I doubt that my family relationships as they existed before the fall would have afforded me the personal or spiritual development that God has effected in me over the past few years. When I think about it, I had no incentive to change given the protections, conveniences, and status quo of our former world. Even more so, I relied more upon my family, than on Christ. My mother helped me figure things out. She was the wisdom source. She told me what thus saith the Lord, so I didn't really have to hear it directly from him. My sister on the other hand, was my justification for whatever and however we were. I was hers as well. Instead of checking each other on our shortcomings and encouraging one another to get better, we celebrated our personal issues believing that they made us the unique specimens we were, and somehow helped us survive in our world. Not! It was just easier to get others to conform to us than to make the appropriate character adjustments for greater compatibility with others. We didn't necessarily make each other better; we simply made each other more secure. Separated, I was able to independently decide what kind of person I wanted to be and relinquish the childhood desire to be more like her. Separated, she was able to accomplish things on her own without respect of me, our family, or our church. Moreover, she no longer had to work so hard to keep me in my place. I was no longer around, no longer a threat. I no longer had a place of significance in her world. She could now carry on without looking over her shoulder. I could carry on without looking to her for direction. We became separate entities who, surprisingly enough, independently thrived.

This is not to say that I'm okay with our new normal, but I'm accepting the reality that God is doing as much of a work in her life as he is in mine. He is orchestrating and maneuvering people, circumstances, and opportunities for her, and is gently leading her to a designated place. It's not for me, or anyone else, to make sense of the past, or try to reconcile it with the present. I remind myself daily that the battle is not mine; it's the Lord's. He is fully capable of fighting it and is guaranteed to get the victory. I believe that he will make all things perfect in his time, according to his will. If he never chooses to fully reconcile my family, I thank him for reconciling each one of us to himself.

We tend to believe that when God delivers us, he does so exclusively for our good. In reality, he shows us favor for one reason: so that *he* can be glorified. He doesn't deliver us, heal us, and restore us just so that we'll be whole again, but rather that we'll be useful for his kingdom. Our victories become our testimonies. Our triumph is someone else's encouragement. Our pain translates into someone else's promise. When the windows of heaven open and pour out blessings that we don't have room for, we're not suppose to move things around to make room…we're suppose to share those blessings with others. That's the purpose of our pain. That's the reason for answered prayers. That's why we're still here.

Even pastor had a purpose in the pain. He has always delivered a sound Word. He's always had a testimony. But in this day and age when so many are grieving, when so many are giving up, when so many can't see their way through, when so many are taking their own lives, when so many are faint in heart, they need to hear him say I've been there, and praise God I survived. Our church family needed to see his tears; not as a means of ridicule, but for the sake of connection. His children needed to see his tears. His sons and daughters alike needed to know that he is not invincible in his own might, he is not immortal, he is not perfect, and he is not God. He is our father. He is human. He feels, he cares, he loves, he hurts, and he heals. For years, he was our invincible hero. He's still our hero. But we appreciate his mortality now, and we cherish his time with us all the more. Thank you, Dad, for letting us see you. Thank you for finally becoming more transparent. Thank you for your example. We've observed. We've learned. We've put into practice, and we, too, have survived.

As for Dad's wife? The Lord gave her a new purpose also: to help save his life; to help restore him to ministry, to be his helpmate, and to re-establish his own purpose. God rapidly seasoned her to be a first lady. And what a seasoning it was! She had to grow thick skin and a heart of forgiveness to survive this storm. Yet, the Lord used this awful experience to ripen her for what he would later do in her marriage, and in her ministry. Even amidst all the chaos, pain, and turmoil, he enabled her to stay focused and caused her to develop the willful transparency needed to please God. I recall her repeating to me a phrase that she had heard not long before, that *God is more interested in our character than in our comfort*. Wow. Can you imagine how impacting our presentation of the Gospel would be if we were all willing vessels to be used however, by what means, and through what suffering, our Creator deemed necessary for his glory? Whether the issue of our heart is loss of a loved one, failure, abuse, depravity, or other matters of life, we have to know that we can, and will, survive. We are children of God, elect of the Sovereign King. Our victory is pre-ordained. We will triumphantly reach the other side of the matter, and our grief will result in his glory. The Bible says, Be thou faithful unto death, and I shall give thee a crown of life (Revelation 2:10, KJV). She has been faithful, and she shall someday receive a crown.

Perhaps the most critical part of our necessary condition was preparation for all that he has in store for the remainder of our lives. There's something to be said for ministry readiness. Our entire journey is one of preparation for the kingdom work that will cause us to draw others closer to Christ, glorify Christ in our existence, and allow him to demonstrate his power and presence in our lives. Our storms provide the crucial preparation that we need so that when the trial comes, we survive! When the enemy comes in like a flood, we recognize the standard! When the weapon is formed, it won't be able to prosper! We're not here for our benefit. We weren't created for our comfort. We're not blessed for blessings' sake. We have a charge, a commission, a call. But how will we ever fulfill it, or even realize it, if we're not sifted, molded, and perfected through his Divine process. How will I ever get reach the place where he wants me to be if I remain stationery? I *must* swim the waters. I *must* go through the fire. I *must* navigate the storm. I *must* climb the mountain. After all, the view is best at the top!

So that's it. That was essentially the whole purpose of the pain. To be ready for our new existence, to be ready for our new commission, to be ready to fulfill our next call. Our pain prepared us for whatever is to come, according to his Will.

The graciousness of God is relentless. Some time after my mom's passing, the Holy Spirit guided me a very insightful scripture: The righteous pass away; the godly often die before their time. And no one seems to understand that God is protecting them from evil to come. For the godly who die will rest in peace. (Isaiah 57:12, RSV) Imagine that. Imagine that the Lord is gracious enough to rescue those that we love from something in their future that would prove more detrimental, more devastating, then the present loss. Imagine that God sees far ahead, and intervenes according to his wisdom and mercy, in the best interest of his children. Imagine if we trusted him.

I implore each Christian resolve one thing at the onset of each trail: we have no choice but to trust him! Don't allow faith to be just an option. Make it a given, an absolute, a conscious choice. Resolve to believe in a deliverance that you can't readily see. Declare your victory at the beginning. Don't wait for the light at the end of the tunnel. Visualize the rainbow now. You know what it looks like, you've seen it before. Let your spiritual eye and your heart's faith see it right now. Don't trust your human sight. Carnal vision is clouded by our limited perception of the situation and distorted by sin. It's not real. It's not the whole story. It's not the end of the matter. Declare to yourself and others at the inception of the thing that Christ has you, that he will bring you through, and that he will perfectly design your destiny in the process. His glory, your good. Trust him.

Recovery, Spiritual Maturity, and Restoration

Let the Healing Waters Flow

There will be times in your journey when you'll have to encourage yourself. You'll have to speak life into your very being in order to change your own mind about your situation. Charles Swindall proclaimed that "Life is 10 percent what happens to you, and 90 percent how you respond." He understood that while we may have little or no control over the circumstances that we find ourselves in, we have absolute control over how we respond. It's that response, positive or negative, which determines our outcome.

It seems lately as if I've been trapped in a cycle of crisis. Even as one storm ends, the atmosphere remains cloudy and yet another storm is imminent. It's terrible to see trouble coming and be helpless to do anything about it. It's even worse when you're so mentally exhausted from the last experience that you don't seem to have the strength, or sense, to take shelter. That's where I've been for quite some time. Just when I think it's safe to go back into the water...

In preparing for our choir's 2007 concert, the Lord led me to Proverbs 18:21a (KJV) which reads, Death and life are in the power of the tongue. He laid on my heart the message that I needed to begin speaking life. Not only did I need to speak life to others, but I needed to speak life to myself. Psychologists and physicians figured this stuff out a long time ago, but we lay people don't fully accept and appreciate the power of the mind. Our mind has the power to rule our mental and physical disposition. The same way we can worry ourselves sick, we can relax ourselves well. The same way negative thoughts that cause depression and distress, positive thoughts can invoke joy and peace. Prayer, faith, and positive thinking are a powerful combination that guarantees formidable results. Healing begins in the mind. Healing of our situation, healing of our bodies, healing of our spirits, and healing of our souls. The Bible says that, so a man thinketh in his heart, so is he (Proverbs 23:7, KJV).

From that day, I began writing words of life on my daily calendar. I write scripture. I write motivational quotes. I write triumphs. (We often forget past triumphs when we enter a new storm, so to remember them, write them down!) I further began the practice of speaking life into others all around me who were going through. Not clichés and void comments, but words of life from the Word of God. I began sharing my testimony, sharing my victories, sharing the things that hindered me from triumph as well as the practices of obedience that the Lord would use to bring me out.

I challenge you to try it. Exchange your sentiment of defeat for an attitude of victory. Then search the Word for scriptures and attributes of God that reaffirm positive outcomes. Finally, pray without ceasing. Pray that you will overcome. Most of all, pray that God will be glorified in your outcome. Speak the promises of God right back to him. Speak his Word out loud. Speak life. God has not given us a spirit of fear, but of power, love and a sound mind! (2 Timothy 1:7, KJV).

Recovery

In CPR class, we're taught to place the victim in recovery position once they regain consciousness and are breathing on their own. Recovery position is one that allows the victim to rest in a safe, comfortable stance while they stabilize and until their vital signs return to normal. In emergency situations, it's the paramedics or physicians that determine when the victim is fully recovered or if additional medical attention is needed. Although the imminent threat has ended, the victim may not quite be out of woods. If he rushes from trauma to normal activity, he will likely have adverse reactions and perhaps even experience a relapse. Recovery position helps ensure wellness.

Similarly, we need to assume a recovery position as we collect ourselves after a crisis. Often times in ministry the temptation is to immediately resume our post, either because we think the Lord would be pleased or because it helps conceal our instability. I learned (again the hard way) that this isn't always a good idea. Actually, it can be a very detrimental move. Our emotional wounds are still wide open and can be easily infected. Our heart is still broken and in need of rest and repair. Our vitals are still out of whack and require time to re-stabilize. And our sanity is always questionable after a crisis! Ministry requires us to be a help to others, to be available to others, to demonstrate the character of Christ. How can we possibly do this if we're still traumatized ourselves! We need a recovery period. Our recovery position should be prostrate before the Lord. Whether we realize it or not, our minds, our bodies, and most of all, our spirits need to rest.

In October 2006, I totaled my husband's car in a four-vehicle accident. I walked away without a scratch, completely in tact, no apparent ailments. As a matter of fact, everyone involved walked away unharmed, praise God. Because there were no visible scars, I thought I was fine. I was *not*. That evening my legs felt a little unstable. By the next morning, my entire back was stiff, my legs were swollen, I had shooting pains in my neck, and I could barely move, let alone walk. It was terrible. I'd bragged the entire day before about how good I felt. Going to the emergency room seemed an unnecessary inconvenience, so I had come straight home from the accident. Needless to say, I had no problem sitting in the emergency room on day two, begging for pain killers and worrying that I might never heal.

Many of our crises are much like car accidents. We miraculously survive, and we come out thanking God for his grace and mercy toward us. There are no visible scars, so we get right back to business as usual. We underestimate the internal damage done, and we fail to consider the aftermath. It's in the post-crisis recovery position that the Lord begins to quietly minister to our spirit. He has our undivided attention without the amplified voices of the outside world. We now have the best opportunity to hear his voice alone, and to respond. It's during this time that he can define for us the purpose of our pain, and begin to refuel and prepare us for the journey ahead. It's an awesome time.

Even amidst all the pain, it's still awesome. No other voice matters, no other opinion matters. You don't have to look a certain way, or behave a certain way, or try to make yourself feel a certain way. You don't have to fix it. He does that for you. He meets you exactly where you are: broken, battered, bruised, and tired. He infuses you with peace while you rest safely in his arms. He calms your spirit, then causes the healing process to begin. After all of my minimally successful self-help techniques, it was sobering to learn that all I had to do was rest, rest in him. He'd take it from there. And he did.

We talked earlier about moving through processes too fast, and I shared that I'm not really big on processes. I'm more of a 'cut-to-the-chase' gal. Wrap it up. Get it done. I have to constantly remind myself that neither crisis nor recovery work that way. Recovery processes, especially, are designed not only to heal, but to reinforce the personal development and spiritual maturity initiated by the crisis in the first place, remember? Depending on where you are in your walk with Christ, and how willing your spirit is to surrender to his will, it can be a sweet journey both during and after the storm. On the other hand, if your objective is solely to get past the pain with no regard for purpose, plans, or spiritual destiny, then buckle up and brace yourself for a painstaking journey!

Consider the Israelites

You've probably heard by now that when the Lord delivered the Israelites from countless years of slavery in Egypt, he intended for them to have a peaceful journey. He must have, because the trip from Egypt to the promised land was only eleven days geographically. Eleven days, that's all. But because of spiritual deficiencies and a lifestyle of disobedience, it took them forty years to reach a destination that God had prepared for them long ago. Wow. It makes you wonder...Where was the GPS System? Tom-Tom, Garvin, something! Why didn't somebody log on to Mapquest and help the poor children out! What was the price of gas back then? Seriously, they must of been traveling in circles. Can you fathom forty years for an eleven-day trip. Lord, help! Forty years of consequences. Forty years of failure. Forty years of reprimand. Forty years of defeat. Forty years of exhaustion. Forty years of confusion. Forty years of complaining. Forty years of sick and tired! Forty years with the same folks, doing the same things, making the same mistakes, learning the same lessons, with the same outcomes. Forty years of pain with no purpose

Just think, many of the Israelites had infant children when they started out who were now adults with children of their own. At the point that your baby's babies are grown, seems like you'd figure some stuff out. Yet, for years they simply didn't get it! They let entire generations grow up without getting it, all due to their own unwillingness to be led by God and submit to his direction. They took their own route, they made their own way, they worked it out for themselves, and consequently, they remained on a perpetual journey to no where.

What must their children have thought of them? What must surrounding nations have thought of them? What damage this must have done to their testimonies. How destructive this was to their faith. Sound familiar? We shame the Israelites, but children of God place themselves in the exact same predicament today. Our children suffer, our testimonies suffer, and the kingdom of God suffers while we travel in needless circles while refusing to heed the voice of God.

Aside from my humor (admit, some of that was really funny!), the moral of the story is *do it God's way the first time*. The crisis and the recovery process will be much sweeter, and probably much shorter!

Spiritual Maturity

The ultimate goal of uncomfortable processes is spiritual maturity. Living well, living wise, living Godly, and getting it right the first time!

In younger years, I had the time, room, and stamina for trial and era living. Time is too precious to waste, though. Whether you're fifteen or fifty, tomorrow is not promised. It's in our best interest to live skillfully today. Why pay the price to take algebra 101 multiple times because you're too lazy or too busy to dedicate the time and energy needed to pass? The school will gladly take your money, but why not strive to pass the first time around and move on to other lessons. For the record, I took algebra several times. But I'm now tired of repeating courses. My goal is to grasp it the first time, even if I have to ask for extra help. I want the Lord to know that he has my full attention, willfully. There may be parts that I don't readily understand, and I may need him to repeat things for clarity every now and again. But I refuse to fail spiritual courses for lack of effort or refusal to follow instructions. I'm just too old for that. It's time to get serious about my spiritual studies so that I can earn a few jewels, a little bling-bling, on my heavenly crown. After all, all the cool Christians will be wearing them!

Also consider this: when we see kids blatantly disrespect their parents in public, our reaction is usually a combination of embarrassment for that parent and ridicule that the parent would allow the child to get so far out of control. Even if it's an isolated incident, we don't know that. We immediately envision a chaotic home life where the child rules the castle while the parent passively looks the other way. The display leaves us with a negative impression of both child and parent, and for those who don't already have kids, they second-guess wanting any now! Well think of the body of Christ, and how we behave while all the world watches. We blatantly disrespect our heavenly Father, and act like unruly ingrates with no kingdom training. It's not only the Christian that looks bad; we cause shame to Christ as well. Unlike the parent who may or may not respond, be assured that the Lord will! One way or another, he'll correct us and bring us into submission. He'll get the glory out of our lives, or at least prevent us doing any more damage to his Name. We're not just going to keep cutting up and embarrassing him over and over again. He'll handle it. Allowing forty years for your silver spooned children to get it together is quite gracious. He could have nipped it in the bud much earlier and revoked their destiny altogether! I wouldn't bank on receiving the same grace periods extended to the Israelites. Besides, most of us don't have forty years! Thank God for his unconditional love, and that his mercy endureth forever. I thank him, also, for a good upbringing and the desire to represent him well.

It's funny how afraid I used to be (and at times I still am) to pray for spiritual things. I remember my mother praying things like, *Lord, have your way in their lives,* or *Lord, draw them closer to you,* or *Lord, bring them into submission to your will by any means necessary.* We'd cringe and ask her to go easy on the militant prayers. We'd suggest that she try using softer. more gentler language such as, *Lord, please guide them gently to the place where you'd have them be without hurt, harm, danger, or inconvenience. And get them a new pair of jeans and tennis shoes along the way, in Jesus Name…* In our minds, the stuff she was praying left us wide open for locusts, famine, and plague!

Even today, many Christians fear the means by which the Lord will get us into his will. As a result, we hesitate to pray accordingly. Well here's a thought: how about getting there voluntarily rather than under duress. What if our children came to us and said, I really want to please you today. May I run some errands, do some chores today, or help you in some other way? (Okay, I know that would never happen, just work with me in the hypothetical realm). Would our response be to beat them, drag them in the bathroom and demand that they start mopping? As a matter of fact, we'd probably feed them and let them play video games for the rest of the day. So why would God's response to our willful submission be to do such things to us? Doesn't it stand to reason that he desires our obedience and would rejoice in obtaining it with ease? Where do we get the idea that we serve a ruthless, iron-fist King who delights in our demise? How does that concept fit in with the sacrifice of Calvary? Inconsistent, at best.

It's hard to accept the unconditional, relentless nature of God's love toward us, because it's impossible to understand. It simply doesn't make sense from a human standpoint. Why would anyone declare unconditional love and forgiveness without strings, or some sort of cost-benefit analysis attached? Nonetheless, he does. Remember, his love is not contingent on our obedience. His forgiveness is not based on the depths of our sin. We must learn to personalize the cross, and the promises in his Word. It's the key to our victory. It's the key to our confidence in praying for and pursuing his will.

In my devotional time, I've been focusing on the obedient figures in the Bible that willingly strived to please the Lord. For example, consider the woman with alabaster box of oil that she voluntarily used to anoint the feet of Jesus. What a positive response she received. He not only defended her in front of the ridiculing crowd, but he blessed her. And what about David? He screwed up something awful. But when he humbled himself and sought the Lord, the Lord delighted in him, covered him, and reconciled David to himself. How about Nicodemus? The Lord spotted him on top of a large crowd trying to do the right thing, called him out, and responded positively to his need. And the woman that proclaimed her healing could come from merely touching the hem of his garment... he blessed her immediately. These and countless other examples confirm that I don't have reason to fear expressing a desire for spiritual maturity, or to wholeheartedly seeking his will for my life. The more intimately we get to know Christ, the less intimidating the relationship with him will be. Communion with him. That's what he wants. It's what he will honor. It's why we're created.

So does this mean that we will avoid pain and suffering by voluntarily submitting to God's will? I'm afraid not. Remember that some of our necessary conditions are for growth, maturity, testimony sake, and to allow for God's glory through our lives-not just to bring us into submission. Yet if we willfully submit to his plan for our lives, we avoid the unnecessary, bitter, consequential part of the process. We avoid the forty years. Our journey is sweeter. Our outcomes are better. Our fellowship is more intimate. Our destination, and our destiny, are assured.

Restoration

Auto collision repair shops typically promise to get your vehicle back to its original condition. And from a naked eye standpoint, they usually do. But you have to be careful of what's under the hood, and what non-visible damage has been done. The vehicle may never again reach its original level of performance, and will certainly not regain its original worth. That's why it's imperative that we don't try to restore ourselves, but rather allow the Lord to do it for us.

Spiritual restoration is threefold, it involves: the Lord restoring unto us the fullness of our joy (Psalms 16:1), the Lord restoring us to our positions and place in the body of Christ, and the Lord reconciling us to himself.

I can't stress enough how crucial it is to let God do the healing, and to allow him to independently guide you though the recovery and restoration processes. We simply can't do it ourselves. There's no over the counter cure. We need prescriptions: the Word of God and the hand of God. It's not a display of weakness to surrender; it's a sign of humility. His strength begins where our resources end.

Until we throw in the towel, we'll continue spinning our wheels and wandering in the dark. We'll expend plenty of energy, but we'll get nowhere.

It's human and natural to fear the unknown and to be uncomfortable in the passenger seat. Unless I'm sleepy, I typically hate the passenger seat. But I'd rather be a blindfolded passenger with Christ as navigator, than to take over the controls and hit yet another brick wall. I've hit countless brick walls, and in case I failed to mention it earlier, those things really hurt! My desire now is to do it his way. A work still very much in progress, I still get it wrong more than I care to admit. But I'm encouraging myself while I encourage you to keep striving. Obedience is so much better than sacrifice.

All that I've shared with you is based on my own pitfalls and outcomes, as well as those that the Lord has allowed me to closely observe. I most certainly don't have all the answers. Yet if I can help even one person avoid that wall, or reduce their heartache, or better serve in the ministry, or be of any practical or spiritual good, then my life experiences have not been in vain.

Once we've been called to the ministry, any ministry ordained by God, quitting is not an option. We're committed until he releases us and moves us on. But from time to time, we may have to set ourselves apart to heal, to refuel, to recover, to be restored, and to increase in spiritual maturity. Our charge is to run the race. We'll finish at different times, and via different courses. Don't get caught up in the details or discouraged by the length of the course. Just allow Christ to be your compass, and run. *Run, Forest! Run*!

So That Not One of These Little Ones Perish

> Take heed that ye despise not one of these little ones; for I say unto you, That in heaven their angels do always behold the face of my Father which is in heaven. Even so, it is not the will of your Father which is in heaven that one of these little ones should perish.
> Matthew 18:10–14 (RSV)

Our greatest opportunity on life's journey is to positively impact the life of a child. The most effective way that we can do that is to lay a biblical foundation for them by educating them in the truth of the Bible, and equipping them with the spiritual and practical tools for success. I mention this because of my passion for youth, and because of my own experiences that taught me the importance of a spiritual framework early on.

In previous chapters I shared various scenarios of our how our relationships and interactions with significant others directly impact our self efficacy. In a day when there is so much destruction, it is absolutely critical that we become the building blocks for our children's world. Society is inundating them with very confusing, detrimental messages about who they are, what they should strive to be, and what they should believe. Our children are struggling with acceptance and identity, and they're trying to find their place of significance by any means necessary. If they can't find positive answers in their home, I assure you they won't stop there. The search will continue, with or without your input.

Working with and for children has been, by far, my most rewarding ministry both in and outside of the church. God has blessed me with a career that gives me daily access to youth from birth through young adulthood. I am continually awed at their intellect, their inquisitiveness, and their resilience to life's unfortunate circumstances. In effect, young children are fresh clay ready and waiting for their world to sculpt them into precious art. They have an innate desire, just like us, to be loved, to belong, and to be directed. They want and need boundaries that will help them properly distinguish between that which is in their best interest versus that which will inhibit their success. Children from all walks of life are screaming for us to pay attention to them: to acknowledge that they exist; to affirm that they matter; to establish why they're here; and to help them find their way. Yet no matter how loud they scream, regardless of how drastically they communicate, we ignore it. We miss it. And then we hold them accountable for failing. The fact is, if they're broken, we broke them. If they're damaged, we damaged them. And if they're lost, it is our charge to find them and guide them safely to the Master.

The church should be a haven for our children. It should cultivate an environment that is safe, consistent, and conducive for their spiritual and practical growth. The church should be accountable for and to its youth. It should mandate accountability from its youth leaders to ensure that these young ones grow in the nurture and admonition of the Lord. We can't afford to take this responsibility lightly. The Bible tells us that it is better that a millstone be tied around our neck and we are thrown in the sea than to harm even one child. Matthew 18:6 (paraphrased). This is evidence that children are close to the heart of God, and that he places great significance on their care.

While the church should provide all the tools at its disposal to facilitate and support the well-being of our youth, it is *not* the church's role to serve as a surrogate parent. We can't rely on the church to raise our children. We can't use the church as a convenient (and free) means of childcare, or passively accept that our children are in good hands and getting all they need to survive. I assure you that they're not. The less involved we are in their church experience, the less impacting the church will be on their spiritual growth, and they're less likely to ever fully engage in Christian living. Moreover, the greater the inconsistency between what children observe us do in church, and what they observe us do at home, the more difficult it will be for them to commit themselves to Christ.

There has to be a balance between church and home. Especially with respect to the time and attention we give to our children and our ministry and the priority that we place on each. On the one hand, parents should be in church with their children. On the other hand, parents have the primary responsibility of nurturing their children and meeting their day-to-day needs. We can't do that if we're always at church. And at the point that our ministry takes apparent precedence over our home, our children are almost guaranteed to resent both us, and the church. I know from whence I speak. Nothing serves as a suitable substitute for our undivided attention: not gifts, not relatives, not activities, not excuses. Youth determine how significant they are through the nonverbal communications of time, attention, and genuine interest in their person. If we're present, they matter. If we're absent (or distracted), they don't. It's quite a simple calculation in their minds. No rocket science needed.

I held lead roles in the majority of our plays at school in my elementary school days (an actress by nature and addicted to the limelight). Additionally, I played piano and bass guitar in our school band starting in the fourth grade. So I was always in one performance or another, all through school, all school-year long. I would be delighted to look out from behind the curtain and see my mother sitting in the audience. She was at every performance and every event. She would always sit near the front, and she would always have the program in hand anxiously awaiting my appearance. While her presence meant the world to me, it was equally disheartening not to see my father. I understood why he wasn't there. Most of our events fell on Wednesday night prayer meeting. He couldn't miss that. Even if they happened to fall on other nights, the church kept him busy seven days a week, fourteen hours per day. It couldn't be helped. He was the pastor. He always made sure that my mom had a way to get there, though, and that we both had a ride home. This was his fix. I understood. I accepted. It hurt. Likewise, I looked forward to his absence at parent-teacher conferences. In fairness, this kind of worked out in my favor, because I'd be home in bed and pretending to be asleep by the time my mom gave him any negative report. I suppose my siblings shared some of these feelings too. My younger brother received numerous wrestling trophies as one of the best wrestlers on the team, undefeated for long stretches of time. I can't recall how many matches my father attended, I'm sure he must have made a few because he was so proud of my brother. For the ones he missed, I'm sure my brother understood and accepted it, and I'd imagine it hurt. We were fortunate enough to have two parents who could stand in the gap for each other. But what if there were only one? And what if there were none?

You'd think my desire for my father's love and support would have made me overly attentive with my child. It didn't. I neglected to give her my undivided attention for a significant portion of her young life. While I attended school events to support her, I was often distracted. I was always working her into my schedule, and on some occasions, openly expressed the inconvenience that the conference, open house, or other event caused me. We communicate these sentiments both out loud and nonverbally, and our children pick them up right away. It pains me to reflect on how she must have felt. It wasn't her fault that school events were scheduled at times that conflicted with other things that I thought to be important. All she knew was that she wanted me to see her artwork on the wall in the classroom, or hear her play the violin. She had no control over when or under what circumstances. And even if she did, how dare I object! How dare I put parameters on *when* she was important, under what conditions, and for how long! How dare I leave her emotionally damaged and attack her self-esteem? I'm her parent. My job is to protect her. My duty is to affirm her. My privilege is to love her. My responsibility is to establish and reinforce her positive self-efficacy. Yet so many times, I failed.

A word of caution, do it while they're young. I spent the better part of my daughter's high school years in make-up mode. When she entered her freshman year, it occurred to me that I'd missed it. I'd missed so much of her growing up. I'd missed so much of her emotional development. She was right there with me, all the time, but I'd managed to miss it. Realizing this, I suddenly went into panic mode. It hit me like a ton of bricks that she'd be leaving my house in less than four years. Had I taught her everything she needed to know? Had I grounded her in the Word of God? Did I set a sufficient example for her? Did I equip her to manage crisis and survive storms? Would she look back over her childhood and resent me? Will she resent the Lord? I had to fix this. So I began over-investing myself in as much of her world as I could. We started spending the majority of our time in one another's space. We confided in one another. We shopped together (okay, we always did that). We exercised together. We worked together. We led the school gospel choir together. We sat in church together. We became co-dependent on one another. It was great. But none of this late in the hour investment overcame years of low self-esteem and lack of identity. None of it countered the paternal rejection that she felt. None of it took back her earlier tears.

When my daughter finally left for college, I grieved severely. The separation was excruciating for both of us.

She had a terrible time adjusting to her new world, and I had a terrible time adjusting to her being gone. Because I'd wasted so much time in her childhood, I focused all my effort in her teen years on attaching her to me, rather than preparing her to depart.

Parents can't be all places at all times. If you're a single parent like I was for sixteen years, God bless you as you try to do it all. You can't. But our job is not to be all things to our children. Our job is to be godly parents. Our charge is to train them up in the Lord, and equip them for life's journey. Equipping them means to establish them, affirm them, and prepare them. We establish them by letting them know where they come from, and giving them a connectedness to a positive world. We affirm them by consistently assuring them that they're loved, that they're valued, that they're significant, and that they have a purpose. We prepare them by teaching them the Word of God, and demonstrating his Word in our own lives; we prepare them by helping them navigate rough waters, praying for them daily, disciplining them along the way, and establishing clear standards for the home and for their lives; we prepare them by covering them, by introducing them to the saving knowledge of Jesus Christ, and by providing an environment that will encourage them to know him for themselves. That's our job. It's awesome. It's rewarding. It's prayerfully achievable.

It Takes a Village, Remember That Old Saying?

We loosely quote the only saying that it takes a village to raise a child, but how many of us become or accept such a village. The truth is, most of us wouldn't tolerate the interference of a village, nor would be risk getting involved in the rearing of another's child. Yet there are so many youth who don't have the support systems and environments needed to positively shape their person, so we as the body of Christ need to become that village. They need us to stand in the gap, to go to their performances, to attend their open houses, to take them to the ball game, to do whatever will give them the practical human supports that they need. Only then have we truly fostered their well-being. Only then are they ripe to hear, receive, and apply the Word of God. Only then is our kingdom work accomplished.

Our church was blessed with such youth pastors and leaders over the years who grasped this need and invested themselves in meeting it. But the harvest has always been plentiful in this regard, and the laborers have always been few. Looking at our present society, the charge to be village caretakers for our youth can seem overwhelming. So I challenge us all not to look at the condition of society, but to look at the power of the cross. We can't impact them all. We won't save every one. But to coin a phrase, each one, touch one. We'll be amazed at the impact. Our Savior will be delighted in our efforts, and he will bless the result.

Ministry Oriented, or Christ Oriented?

Since I can remember, I've always loved to write, and I've always had some sort of story to tell. Yet this book sat in my mind and heart for twenty years. Revelation: the primary reason why the book was not completed until now was that God did not intend for my writing passion to be about telling good stories; he gave it to me as a means of sharing my testimony. Twenty years ago, my testimony had not been fully realized. Twenty years ago, I hadn't experienced the necessary conditions that would serve to mature me spiritually, and help me strengthen my brethren. Even ten years ago, the book would have been solely about life in the ministry, but not about life with Christ.

As a child, I served in church to please my father. As a young adult, I served to please the congregation. My service has always been for some altruistic reason wherein I was fulfilling my perceived duty rather than operating in accordance with my call. I'm not the only one. Pastoral families, particularly first families of a church, have an inbred sense of duty that is impressed upon them early on and consistently reinforced throughout their lives. Serving as ministry leaders is our role. It's what we're expected to do. It's what comes natural for us. It's what makes us significant in our world. It's who we become. We serve out of obligation; we serve in restitution; we serve as a distraction; we serve out of habit; we serve under duress; we serve out of love for our parents; we serve in admonition of our pastor; we serve as a cover; we serve for the benefits; we serve in obedience to the scriptures; we serve in obedience to the bible. We even serve out of genuine love for others. We serve, and our lives are governed by our service.

There's no fault in most of these motivations. The critical error is that none of them are centered on Christ. I was recently listening to the prayer of a psalmist who requested that God *pick her, choose her*. In return, she vowed to *live her life as a thank you*. That's should be the motivation for ministry… living our lives as a thank you!

We've been taught so many reasons for doing right. Some of us do right for right's sake. That's marvelous. Yet these lessons seem to focus on the cost-benefit analysis of Christian living: living out of the will of God will cost you, and living according to the will of God will benefit you. He'll open up the windows and pour out blessings that you won't have room for. This is true. He will. The Bible says so. But that's not why we should minister. It should not be the sole reason why we serve.

We tend to want to offer sacrifices to God. But the Bible says that *obedience* is better than sacrifice (1 Samuel 15:22). More than anything, the Lord delights in our thankfulness. He enjoys our praise. He created us to worship. The breath of life was given for the sole purpose of using it to glorify him. Let everything that hath breath praise the Lord! For us to place priority on any other reason for service is not only misguided, but it robs God of his investment in his creation. It miscommunicates his intention. It undermines his design of our person. It causes us to fall short of his perfect plan for our lives.

Throughout the Word of God, he creates, establishes, and ordains for a distinct reason. Everything he touches has a purpose: whether human or beast; whether firmament or plant; whether light or dark. Everything has a purpose. Even ministries were established with specificity. The Levites were given detailed instructions for worship: the time, the place, and the method by which they would minister were deemed by God. He is a skillful administrator and a masterful architect. He designs everything perfectly. Perfectly, and with a purpose.

When God the Father sacrificed God the Son on Calvary, he did so with a contingency: that the Son must be our means of access to the throne. The Bible says that No one cometh to the Father, but by Me (John 14:6, KJV). Thus, if Christ is the focus of our salvation, why wouldn't he be the focus of our call, the focal point of our ministry? What other reason could justifiably supersede glorifying Christ with respect to why we serve?

With My Whole Heart

The Bible frequently uses the term, with all my heart or with my whole heart. We even use it a lot in church. We sing and pray these words often. We proclaim to love the Lord with all of our heart. That we'll worship him with all our heart. When I read a similar passage recently in the Book of Psalms, a revelation pierced my very being: That's it, that's my problem. That's the essence of my insecurity, the reason for my deficiency, the cause of my fatigue, the source of my discouragement, the mundaneness of my worship. *I have not given God my whole heart.* I thought I had, I desired to, but I haven't done it. I haven't even tried.

The Word of God tells us to guard our affections because they govern everything else in our lives. What our heart is most concerned with, or most strongly attached to, is what will drive our existence. Our heart's affections will define our person. Our affections rule our actions, our justifications for our actions, our lifestyle, our service, our testimony, our spiritual state, our relationship with Christ, our relationship with others, our very being. Here's the scary part. Not only must we guard are affections, but we must take caution in even trusting our affections. The Bible goes on to say that, *the heart is deceitful above all things, and desperately wicked. Who can know it?* (Jeremiah 17:9, KJV). This tells me not only don't I fully understand my own heart, but left to its own devices, it will precipitate my destruction! Wow. It's my sinful nature that governs my heart. It's my sinful nature that establishes my affections. It's my sinful nature that forcefully guides my heart away from Christ, toward unimaginable dangers. No wonder he warns us to be on guard! No wonder he offers a specific solution-the only solution-to give our hearts fully and completely to God. Not only does he desire our undivided adoration, he knows that only in his hands are our hearts protected. Only with him, are our hearts safe. Only with him can our hearts be whole, well, and fully functional.

As the Lord revealed this me, he caused me to examine the condition of my own heart. I began to reflect back over my life and recall all the times my heart had been broken. I recalled all the places I invested my heart; all the people I gave jurisdiction over my heart; all the things I left my heart vulnerable to; all the times that my heart led me to untold danger, and inexplicable hurt. I remembered the many times that pursuing my heart's desires almost resulted in my demise. I realized the extent to which my heart has separated me from God. I acknowledged that he'd never before had my whole heart, and that it is crucial that I give it to him right now.

The main reason why we struggle so much in ministry and in our personal lives is that we are constantly expending effort to protect and preserve the well-being of our hearts. In relationships, we freely give our hearts to others and hold them accountable for taking good care thereof. We make others responsible for making our hearts happy, and we want to crucify them when they fail. We even go so far as to communicate this sentiment to our loved ones. *I trusted you with my heart, I gave you all of me, and look what you did! Look how you betrayed me! How could you do this to me?* The answer is quite simple actually, human beings shouldn't be entrusted with the care of your heart! They can't even govern their own. God has not given us competency in this area, intentionally so. He never intended us to give our whole hearts to man. I can love you, unconditionally. But my heart, the essence of my being, must belong to God.

Ministry is conceivably one of the leading heartbreakers among Christians, especially among spiritual leaders. It's where individuals tend to invest themselves to the fullest extent, with the lease amount of caution, in anticipation of the greatest reward. We tend to seek affirmation for our investment, and we naively trust our hearts, our very beings, to our ministry environments and those therein. We justify this phenomenon because it's related to the work of the Lord. We're doing it on his behalf, per his command. Really? When did the Lord command us to give our whole hearts to the ministry? Where in the Bible are we instructed to abandon all for the sake of the church, or to take up our cross and follow the people of God. Such commands are not written. Every command that God gives us regarding ministry, servitude, or even love is given with an emphasis on glorifying the Lord and honoring him. Thus, ministry should have no jurisdiction over our hearts. Our souls don't belong to the church. Our fellowship in the church and our role in ministry should be a result of the commitment of our heart to Christ, and Christ alone. He can protect it. He can preserve it. He can glorify himself though it.

Consider this: people and circumstances can only have a limited impact on your heart, positive or negative, if your heart is given wholly to God. If on Sunday morning, I am truly worshiping God with my whole heart, there's no room for anything else to take up space. If in my home I'm worshiping God with my whole heart, there's no room for me to worship my husband, my children, my possessions. Thus, there's limited opportunity for them to distract my focus. I can, and I must, honor them, nurture them, and love them unconditionally. I may have even heard some interesting language in our marital vows suggesting that I should *cherish and obey*. I'll reluctantly agree to work on that! But to the extent that they fail to reciprocate, to the extent that they fall short of meeting my human needs for unconditional love, affection, and affirmation (and believe me, they will), the impact of their shortcoming should be minimal as my heart is in the hand of God. Of course I'll be disappointed. Of course, I'll be hurt. But imagine if my heart is still intact, because all along it was in God's hands!

So let's review, the more my heart belongs to God, the less occasion it has to be broken by others. The more my focus is centered on Christ, the less the chance of being wounded by circumstance; less likelihood of being discouraged; and it will be virtually impossible for my heart to be destroyed. Hmmm. Sounds like a pretty sound investment.

Think of it this way: if the heart is the essence of our being, and God is a jealous God that desires our essence, then it stands to reason that the only means by which we can truly please him is by giving him our whole heart. Not our time, not our service, not our words, but our whole heart. In doing so, we will more successfully fulfill our ministry office, and more effectively respond to our call.

There is nothing more that you can give of yourself than your heart. There's no more complete commitment. There's no greater cost. Why entrust anyone other than the Creator with the essence of his creation? Given the blessed transformation on our lives when we surrender only a small portion of our being to him, imagine the extraordinary things he could accomplish through us if we committed to him our whole heart

Who I Am, In Christ

The time has come for me to relinquish the emotional and practical significance of my birthright as the pastor's daughter. It's time that I begin to celebrate, instead, my birthright and a child of God. I adore my dad, he's now one of the closest people to me, and the closest connection to my mom that I have here on earth. He's my hero. But my call is no longer attached to him. I now have a call, an appointment, of my own. One that, Lord willing, will reach beyond the walls of our church, and beyond the constraints of my childhood. I believe that the Lord will soon take me out of my comfort zone altogether and set me in a new place where my gifts will make room, and I can fully realize his vision for my life.

Today, I still serve with a small sense of indebtedness, a sense of restitution, a sense of endearment for my beloved father, my pastor, and out of sheer obedience. Yet my heart's utmost desire is to please God. I desire to please him in my life; I desire to please him in my work; I desire to please him in my parenting; I desire to please him in my marriage; I desire to please him in my Christian walk. I want every encounter that I have with others to be such that they see the Jesus in me. I want to minister to others in such a way that their lives are never again the same: not because of me, but because of Christ within. I pray that my life's experiences and the lessons that I've learned will serve as an enlightenment, an encouragement, and a supportive rope that stabilizes others as they climb their own spiritual mountain. When you get past the roughness and finally approach the top, remember all that God has done, and live your life as a Thank you.

For only a little while longer, I'll be known as the pastor's daughter. For eternity, I'll be known as a child of the King.

The Legacy

Within a few days of this book's completion, Dr. Eddie L. Hawkins will formally retire as founding pastor of Good Shepherd Baptist Church, after fifty years of faithful service.

He'd contemplated doing so years earlier, especially when my mother went home to glory in 2002. Retirement rumors have always circulated, and many suspected that this day was coming, but there was nothing that could have prepared the congregation to actually hear the words from his mouth, and be faced with processing the reality of his departure. Unlike many churches, we've never known such transition. We've had the same pastor since inception: the same godly standard, the same sound doctrine, the same protocol, the same culture, the same relationship, the same tradition. We never had to wonder what box minister would come out of, what new fad our church body would succumb to, or what our pastor's position would be on various matters. We always knew. We had consistency, we had clarity, we had stability, and we had a covering. We took great pride in knowing that as a body, our church stood on a solid foundation. We seemed to be less susceptible to changing tides, because our leadership was not influenced by peers, or by the world. This is not to say that individual members didn't often fall victim to societal norms, but within the walls of our church home, the standard prevailed over changing norms. We stood on the Word of God, and honored the house of God.

We're now preparing to celebrate his ministry legacy: fifty years that my father has led our church congregation, fifty years of getting the Word of God to the people, fifty years of service, fifty years of sacrifice, fifty years of blessings, fifty years of an awesome legacy!

Pastor described his impending retirement as a death. He says it feels very similar to losing your closest loved one, and that the grieving process is much the same. This ministry is his conception; it's his legacy; it's been his lifeblood for five decades. It's why he got up in the morning, and what he contemplated when he went to bed at night. It was the sustaining force in his marriage, in his family, in his Christian life, in his existence. It's how he defined himself, his purpose, his passion. It's what he loved, what he was committed to, what he nurtured, what he could impact, what he could build. It's how he served the Lord. It's how he measured his contribution to the kingdom. It's how he honored his Master. It's how he carried out the plans of his Father. This ministry defined his path in life, and the paths of his family. Since birth, my family and I were not only groomed for our roles in ministry, but he instructed us with regard to or our ministry's end at our home church. We understood that if and when my father's leadership work ended at the church, so would ours. Not because we were there for his sake, but to ensure that we did not undermine the authority of the new pastoral family, or stand in the way the new vision and direction that God would give the new leaders. The problem is that we never really contemplated this end, so we weren't cognitively or emotionally prepared for it. This was our foundation, our Christian environment, our fence, our home.

Like with any move, this one is hard. We don't feel like packing, and we definitely can't process saying goodbye. In recent months, I've secretly stood in the doorway and observed my father slowly pacing aisles of our sanctuary. He'd appear to be in deep thought, or maybe praying. Then all of a sudden, he'd stop, sit down, and then stare out of the full view windows at our church campus with his elbow on the back of the seat and hand on his chin. Still silent, still pondering, still praying. I remember thinking to myself that this really is like death...this is the exact same thing he did during my mom's illness, and when he returned from leave after her home going. I tried to imagine what he must be feeling at that moment. I wondered if he was approaching resolve, gaining closure, or perhaps struggling with the finality of his decision. I wondered if he had an inkling of what the Lord had in store for him next, or what his life would be like the day after the last day here. I saw him wipe tears, I simultaneously wiped my own. I saw him look toward heaven as if to say, not my will, Lord, but Thine. So I, too, looked toward heaven and prayed that the Lord would continue to anoint my father afresh, and be ever glorified in his life. After what seemed like hours, he was still sitting by himself in the sanctuary. Yet, I suddenly felt an awesome peace, and realized that he wasn't alone. The Spirit of the Lord spoke to me and assured me that my father was in the presence of the Lord, and that there was nothing for me to do, except walk away and leave them to commune. So I left without ever being noticed by my father, and without ever mentioning to him these phenomenal moments that I had observed. Never did I tell him how this silent experience, together with the numerous times before that I'd seen him quietly worship, study, and seek the face of the Lord, tremendously impacted my life. I never told him. But I'll always revere him for it. And I'll never forget that day.

Human nature resists change. Even someone like myself, who has an extremely restless spirit and constantly seeks the next venture, is hesitant to embrace unsolicited change. As weary as I've become over the years, as much as I've anticipated the day when my life would no longer be defined by our ministry, I am deeply grieving this change. I can't imagine any other life. None of us can fathom the emotional, spiritual, and practical impacts of this change. I guess that's where faith comes in.

The Lord says in Jeremiah, I know the plans I have for you; plans for good and not for evil, to give you a future and a hope (Jeremiah 29:11, KJV). He also tells us in Jeremiah 33:3 (KJV), Call unto me and I will answer thee, and shew thee great and mighty things which thou knowest not. I believe that even after all these years of ministry, after all these years of service, God still has a very specific and definitive plan for my father's life. God is not finished with him yet. Even for the rest of my family, I am confident of this very thing, that he which hath begun a good work in [us] will perform it until the day of Jesus Christ (Philippians 1:6, KJV).

My mother firmly believed in her heavenly Father's plan for all of our lives. She was persuaded that nothing happens by chance, and that nothing takes place without the Lord's divine or permissive appointment. She was confident that her family is called according to his purpose, and she rested in the faith that the Lord would affect our good, for his glory.

The Lord is already fulfilling his promises in our lives. My older sister is continuing in ministry at her own church. We're slowly mending the scars of our relationship, and bonding our family back together. My younger brother is impacting countless lives in our community and our world through his political contributions and service. I believe God will use him to evoke practical and spiritual change not only in our communities but in our world! He is awesome. My older brother has a uniquely close relationship with my father, and continues to be his rope holder and confidante. He remains in the financial industry, but I suspect that the Lord has a higher calling on his life. I further suspect that he knows it. Me, I'm writing the vision.

So you see, ministry doesn't end with a particular tour of duty. Ministry ends when we get to Glory. Until then, we are compelled to fulfill our call. Once a pastoral family, always a pastoral family. Once a Christian, always a Christian. Once committed to Christ, please be committed always! Kingdom work has no expiration, no specific lifespan. It has no limits. It has no boundaries. It has no impossibilities. What God ordains, he will maintain. I have no doubt that this end will transform into a new beginning for us all. Have thine own way, dear Lord, have thine own way.

Be careful what you pray, and trust that the Lord will answer for his glory. I say this because during final edits of this book, our lives dramatically changed - again. Just when my family and I thought it was safe to go back in the water, we found ourselves in the eye of another storm. We've entered the wilderness — again. Our testimonies are being called upon — again. This time, God has commanded a crisis in the life of the Politician to not only affect healing and reconciliation in our family, but also to draw countless people closer to Christ. Wow. His ways never cease to amaze me! Once again, we're adjusting to a new kind of normal. Yet will we trust him. Yet will we praise him. Yet will we rest in the assurance that our *Father Planned it All*.

Our lives are testaments to the fact that the Lord can use anyone, in any situation, under any circumstance, and for any period of time to glorify himself. It's not about us. It's not about our pleasure, it's not about our pain, it's not about our security, it's not about our success. At the end of the day, it is truly all about Christ!

Dearest Daddy,

(It should be okay to call you that now; we're temporarily off the clock!):

> If you're reading these pages, praise God, my prayers have been answered! Know that you have forever imprinted the lives of our congregation and permanently impacted each life you touched. You have served successfully, by God's standard, and through your distinguished life, you have represented the Savior well. You are a blessing. Even the angels must stand amazed at such a man, with such a heart for their Creator. You have honored Christ in your ministry, and in your living. You have fought an extraordinary fight, you have kept an uncompromising faith, and you have stood firmly on the Word of God. I have no doubt that when you see the face of Jesus, he will say, Well done, my good and faithful servant. Well done. On behalf of your flock, and your family, w*e love you, and well done.*

Remembering Norma Jean Hawkins in love.